SOLIHULL
PAST

View of High Street from the roof of Silhill House, 1911, decorated for the Coronation of George V.

SOLIHULL PAST

Sue Bates

Phillimore

2001

Published by
PHILLIMORE & CO. LTD.
Shopwyke Manor Barn, Chichester, West Sussex

ISBN 1 86077 176 9

Printed and bound in Great Britain by
BIDDLES LTD.
Guildford, Surrey

In Loving Memory
of
Kathleen Hird
1914-2001

Contents

List of Illustrations ix

Acknowledgements xii

Introduction xiii

1. The Beginning, Geography and Agriculture 1

2. Trade and Industry 14

3. Transport 31

4. Religion 41

5. Education 52

6. Public Service 65

7. Houses 81

8. Social Life, Events and Entertainment 94

9. Solihull in Wartime 109

10. Epilogue 122

Notes 123

Bibliography 125

Index 127

List of Illustrations

Frontispiece: View of High Street from the roof of Silhill House, 1911

1. Bridge over River Blythe, c.1910 1
2. Streetsbrook Road, Solihull, 1900 2
3. The 'wyches oak', c.1900 3
4. Manor House Farm, Olton, c.1910 4
5. King Henry III 5
6. Church Hill, Solihull, 1909 5
7. Blossomfield Road, Solihull, c.1900 6
8. Malvern Park Farm, Solihull, 1892 7
9. Harvesting in Lugtrout Lane 8
10. Mrs. Warner feeding piglets 8
11. Mrs. Warner, Lugtrout Lane 9
12. John Markham at Whar Hall Farm 9
13. Bill Markham at Whar Hall Farm 10
14. Farming at Malvern Park Road 10
15. Harvesting in St Bernard's Road 11
16. Foredrove Farm, 1920 11
17. Dovehouse Farm, c.1930 12
18. George Beck from Malvern Park Farm . . 12
19. H. Morgan, Manor Farm 13
20. The Saddlers Arms, pre-1899 14
21. High Street, 1829 15
22. High Street, 1853 16
23. Mann's Curio Shop 17
24. High Street, 1897 17
25. High Street, c.1907 18
26. Silhill House and shops, c.1912 19
27. High Street, c.1910 20
28. Lea's grocer's shop, High Street 20
29. Bragg's butcher's shop, 1908 21
30. Bourne's Seed Merchants, 1930s 22
31. Warwick Road, c.1908 22
32. Marshall's ironmonger's shop 23
33. Poplar Road, c.1930 24
34. Olton Windmill, Lode Lane, 1897 25
35. Henwood Watermill, c.1925 26
36. Tanyard cottages, Warwick Road 26
37. Solihull Brickworks, Warwick Road 27
38. W. Colley (builders) in Drury Lane 28
39. Dixon's timber yard, pre-1937 28
40. Vehicle at Wilsdon & Co 29
41. Water engineering 29
42. R.G. Boardman Ltd., Lode Lane 30
43. Warwick Road 31
44. George Hotel, c.1863 32
45. Excursion from Solihull, c.1900 33
46. Warwick & Birmingham Canal 34
47. Solihull railway station, post-1902 34
48. Construction on Great
      Western Railway 35
49. Bertie Gray and pony, c.1880s 35
50. Unknown riders 36
51. Dr. Edward Sutton Page 36
52. Unknown lady in pony cart 37
53. Ledbrook's Great Western Mews 37
54. Traffic in the High Street, c.1910 38
55. Children with bicycles, c.1910 38
56. Dr. Adolphus Bernays with
      Joseph Fripp, 1907 39
57. Motor accident at junction of Warwick
      Road and Ashleigh Road, 1914 39
58. Motor coach at Wilsdon & Co, 1920s . . 40
59. Roger's Garage 40
60. St Alphege Church, c.1240 41
61. St Alphege Church, c.1900 42
62. St Alphege Church, pre-1921 42
63. St Alphege Church, interior, c.1858 43
64. St Alphege Church, interior 44
65. The Rev. T.B. Harvey Brooks 45
66. St Alphege Church Choir, c.1903 45
67. St Augustine's Church, pre-1904 46
68. St Augustine's Church, interior 47
69. Members of St Augustine's Church 48
70. Bethesda Chapel, Union Road 48
71. Solihull Congregational Church 49
72. Original Methodist Chapel,
      Blossomfield Road, 1982 50
73. Solihull Methodist Church,
      Blossomfield Road, 1983 50
74. Gospel Hall, Poplar Road, 1982 51
75. Malvern House, c.1900 52
76. Solihull School, Warwick Road 53
77. Dining Room, Solihull School 54
78. Dormitory, Solihull School 54
79. First Hockey XI, Solihull School 55

80. Park Road School   56
81. Park Road School—infants, c.1930s   56
82. Park Road School—girls, c.1910   57
83. Park Road School—teachers, c.1930s . . .   57
84. Mill Lane Boys' School, 1960   58
85. Mill Lane Boys' School, football team . .   58
86. Sharmans Cross School, 1934   59
87. Solihull High School for Girls,
      Malvern Hall, c.1934   60
88. Art Room, Solihull High School
      for Girls, c.1930   60
89. Library, Solihull High School
      for Girls, c.1930   61
90. Assembly Hall and gym, Solihull High
      School for Girls, c.1930   61
91. The Priory, Church Hill, c.1890   62
92. Private school in Warwick Road   63
93. Eversfield Preparatory School   64
94. Old Town Hall, The Square   65
95. Solihull Rural District Council, 1916 . . .   66
96. Mr. A.E. Currall, Surveyor   67
97. Solihull Rural District Council   68
98. Council House, Poplar Road   69
99. General Election results, 1951   69
100. Princess Margaret and Councillor
      R.D. Cooper, Charter Day, 1954   70
101. Last Council meeting in the old
      Council House, 1968   71
102. Village water pump in Drury Lane   72
103. Solihull Gas Works, Wharf Lane   73
104. Solihull Gas Works, c.1950   74
105. Solihull Fire Brigade with trophies from
      inter-district championship, c.1935   75
106. Fire at the Hermitage, Lode Lane   76
107. Superintendent Carbis and
      Solihull Police, 1920   77
108. Harvey Chattock (1819-98)   77
109. Doctor's House, Warwick Road   78
110. Dr. Ferdinand Page   78
111. Welfare Food Campaign, 1953   79
112. Solihull Clinic, Drury Lane, 1960   80
113. Evans Convalescent Home,
      Widney Manor Road   80
114. Nos. 7-9 Hampton Lane, c.1956   81
115. Silhill Hall, Streetsbrook Road   82
116. Conjectural drawing of Silhill Hall
      by J.A. Cossins, c.1890   82
117. Libbards House, c.1970   83
118. Solihull Rectory, pre-1933   83
119. High Street with the Manor House   84
120. High Street, c.1910   85
121. Touchwood Hall, Drury Lane   87
122. Cottages in Park Road, pre-1931   88
123. Cottages in Warwick Road   88
124. Cottage in Warwick Road   89
125. Poplar House, c.1900   89
126. Villas in Warwick Road, c.1916   90

127. Mr. and Mrs. Cull and family in
      Lugtrout Lane, c.1910   90
128. 'Church View', School Lane, c.1910   90
129. Typical parlour maid, c.1910   91
130. 'Hazlewood', Homer Road, 1913   91
131. No.3 Lode Lane, pre-1964   92
132. No.739 Warwick Road, c.1956   92
133. No.86 Alston Road, interior   93
134. No.86 Alston Road   93
135. Temporary 'prefab'—No.8
      Jasmine Lane, 1950s   93
136. May Day, 1878   94
137. A circus in the Square, c.1910   95
138. The Matthews family, c.1890   96
139. Brueton Park, c.1953   97
140. Solihull Reading Room & Library,
      High Street, c.1896   98
141. Fancy dress dance at the Public Hall   99
142. Solihull Flower Show, c.1905 100
143. Garden Party in Ashleigh Road 100
144. The Oddfellows at the George Hotel 101
145. The Mothers' Union 101
146. Solihull Carnival, 1935 101
147. The Golden Lion, c.1897 102
148. The Gardener's Arms, 1904 103
149. Solihull Bowling Green, George Hotel . . . 104
150. Solihull Football Club, 1921 106
151. The Fire Brigade and procession,
      Queen Victoria's Diamond Jubilee . . . 106
152. High Street, 1911 107
153. Pensioners celebrating the Coronation
      of Queen Elizabeth II, 1953 107
154. Unknown wedding, c.1910 108
155. Unknown wedding reception 108
156. The Rev. C.O.R. Wormald 110
157. Members of the Harrison family
      with an unknown rifleman 111
158. Members of the Edginton family at
      the wedding of an unknown trooper . 111
159. War widow Mrs. Harriet Davis with
      Blanche and John 112
160. Wounded soldiers at the Hermitage,
      Lode Lane 112
161. Dedication of the War Memorial 113
162. Barrage balloon team 114
163. Mr. and Mr. Robinson's wedding 115
164. Entertaining the crew of HMS Vivacious
      in the Public Hall, March 1944 115
165. Mrs. Herraty inspecting components
      at the Rover Aero Factory 116
166. Short Stirling bomber at Austin Aero
      works at Elmdon 117
167. Home Guard at the Rover
      works, 1941 117
168. Roy Townsend at No.41 Elementary
      Gliding School, Knowle 118
169. Opening of the British Restaurant 119

170. Celebrating American aid 119
171. Wilbur Matheson and John Werthman
        visiting Dorchester Road 120

172. VJ Party in Ulleries Road, Olton 121

Illustration Acknowledgements

Solihull Collection (Solihull Library), 1-4, 7-8, 16, 26, 28, 30-5, 37, 42-3, 46-7, 56, 59-61, 64, 67-8, 72-8, 80, 84, 87-90, 93, 95, 97-100, 109, 112-3, 115-6, 118-20, 123-4, 126, 131, 137, 140, 143, 146, 149, 152, 161, 164, 169-70; Author, 5, 21, 63; Joiner Collection (Solihull Library), 6, 20, 22-3, 24-5, 27, 29, 41, 45, 48, 62, 71, 91, 94, 101, 106, 108, 121, 136, 147-8, 151; Mrs. D. Mason, 9, 10,11, 133-4; Mrs. Dalloe, 12-3; Mrs. R. Smith, 14, 55, 69; St Margaret's Church, Olton, 15, 49, 138; *Solihull News*, 17; Mr. E. Hands, 18; Dr. D. Gray, 19, 50, 52, 54, 57, 127-9, 154-5, 157-8; Miss Freeman, 36, 38; Mr. Wyatt, 39; *Wilsdon & Co*, 40, 58; Warwick Record Office, 44, 70, 122; Mr. Price, 51, 110; Mr. T. Warner, 53, 82, 85, 144; Mr. W. Campbell Smith, 65-6, 125, 130; Mr. M. King, 79; Mrs. Thurston, 81; Mrs. Hawker, 83; Mr. George, 86; Mrs. Hatton, 92; Miss J. Currall, 96; Mrs. Paddock, 102; Mr. A. Saddler, 103; Dr. Bob Cockerham, 104; Mr. Baker, 105; Mr. T. Clark, 107; Mr. D. Patterson, 111; Mr. S. Jones, 114; Solihull M.B.C., 117; Mr. R. Caulfield, 132; Mrs. Frederiks, 135; Mrs. Ruth Chase, 139; Mrs. Johnson, 141; Mrs. Shaw, 142; Miss A. Reynolds, 145; Mr. Hurst, 150; Mr. Pountney, 153; St James' Church, Shirley, 156; Mrs. Baker, 159; Mr. J. Marks, 160; Mr. Collier, 162; Mr. Robinson, 163; Mrs. Herraty, 165; Mr. Woodcock, 166; Mr. Blissett, 167; Mr. R. Townsend, 168; Miss. B. Rolfe, 171; Mrs. G. Arnold, 172.

Acknowledgements

I would like to thank all those who have helped me in my research for this book, which is the result of many years work as Local Studies Librarian at Solihull Library. It is impossible to name everyone here but special thanks are due to the late Charles Lines for the information he always shared so generously and to Joy Woodall for her constant help and support. I am also grateful to my colleagues in the Information & Local Studies Department at Solihull Library and in particular to Paula Murdoch for additional research, and to my partner Noel Hird for help with research and for his continued support.

Introduction

Solihull was founded as a new town in the 12th century by the lords of the manor of Ulverlei and situated in the ancient Forest of Arden. Initially a successful market town, it declined during the 14th and 15th centuries following economic crises caused by poor harvests, the large death rate during epidemics, and competition from several other markets in the vicinity.

By the 17th century Solihull had become a quiet village, typical of many such communities in Britain. The parish was large and encompassed Catherine-de-Barnes, Copt Heath, Bentley Heath, Shirley and part of Olton.

The 18th century witnessed the introduction of turnpike roads which brought some custom to the town's coaching inns but it was the arrival of the railway in the mid-19th century which eventually changed the character of the town completely. The railway opened the way for commuters from neighbouring Birmingham and during the next 150 years the countryside around Solihull gradually disappeared under housing developments.

In the last 50 years of the 20th century Solihull town developed as a commercial centre with shopping and office developments, business parks and hotels all taking advantage of the town's situation at the centre of the national motorway and rail network and the proximity of Birmingham International Airport.

This book is intended to offer a glimpse into the town's history and bring some of that past to life with the help of a selection of old photographs and the eye-witness accounts of former residents. I have attempted to use illustrations which have not been published before (though this is not always possible) and my intention was to produce a companion volume to *Solihull: a pictorial history*.

Sue Bates
February 2001

One

The Beginning, Geography and Agriculture

Solihull is situated on the Midland plateau and most of its undulating landscape is four to five hundred feet above sea level with the shallow valley of the River Blythe to the east. There is a gradual ascent to the south west leading to a ridge at Forshaw. The soil is mainly clay and a lighter sand with some gravel.

The River Blythe rises at Earlswood Lakes, which are artificial reservoirs constructed in the 1790s to feed the *Stratford Canal*. The river's name derives from Old English and means quiet, slow-moving or calm flowing; it was first recorded in the reign of Henry II.

The Blythe follows a meandering course for about twenty-two miles, passing Monkspath, Solihull, Ravenshaw, Temple Balsall, Barston and Hampton-in-Arden, before joining the River Cole near Coleshill. The Cole almost immediately joins the River Tame which in its turn merges with the River Trent and flows eventually into the River Humber so that water from the Solihull area reaches the North Sea after a long journey north.

1 Bridge over River Blythe, Warwick Road, Solihull, *c.*1910.

2   Streetsbrook Road, Solihull, 1900.

Several brooks and streams join the Blythe along its route (which is almost entirely within the present Metropolitan Borough of Solihull). The Cran Brook joins the river near Monkspath, followed by the Alder Brook in Solihull, the Cuttle Brook near Dorridge, and Eastcote Brook near Barston. Approximately seventy per cent of the ground water in the Solihull area is carried away by the river and its tributaries, including the treated water from Barston Sewage Works which reaches the Blythe via Eastcote Brook.

The Blythe is very rich in botanical terms. A variety of plants appear along its course including marsh marigold, common clubrush, yellow water lily and branched burweed. The river and its banks have been designated a Site of Special Scientific Interest (SSSI) by the Nature Conservancy Council and are now subject to many regulations to protect their environment.

The Solihull area was originally deciduous woodland consisting of trees such as oak, elm and ash, with some areas of open heathland, and lay within the Forest of Arden. Place-names offer evidence for these features of the landscape : the ending 'lei' in Ulverlei and Shirley means 'clearing' (by implication in the woodland) and Lode Heath, Elmdon Heath, Copt Heath and Catherine-de-Barnes Heath remain to indicate some of the heaths.

The Arden was a wooded plateau covering much of the north-west part of Warwickshire. The south-east part of the county known as the Feldon was less wooded and offered good opportunities for agriculture from an early date.

It is likely that hunter-gatherers visited the plateau in the Stone Age, and recent finds at Barston suggest that by the Mesolithic period temporary camps were being used here. Evidence in the Knowle area points to Bronze-Age farming and by around 700BC Celts had appeared in the vicinity of the plateau.

There were no major Roman roads in the Solihull area but there may have been a minor road near Solihull to link forts at Birmingham and Coventry. There is no evidence of any significant Roman town near Solihull although there were settlements, probably for agriculture, and there have been finds of pottery and coins in Olton, Solihull, Barston and Eastcote (where a Romano-British field system has been discovered).

The sudden Roman withdrawal from Britain in the early 5th century AD was followed by invasions of Angles and Saxons from across the North Sea. Some settlers arrived in the Arden along the valleys of the rivers Trent and Tame.

The combination of heavy soil and woodland would have made the area unattractive to settlers by the Anglo-Saxon period because agriculture would have been difficult. It is not surprising, therefore, to see that the area was still sparsely populated by the time of the Domesday Survey of 1086. Two manors are shown in Domesday Book in the area which eventually became the parish of Solihull. Both were founded in the Anglo-Saxon period and Ulverlei was a

3 The 'wyches oak', Warwick Road, Solihull, *c.*1900.

large manor with its centre in present-day Olton, while Longdon was smaller and was situated on a low ridge running south west from Catherine-de-Barnes to Bentley Heath.

The population of Ulverlei has been estimated at around 150[1] and it was held by Cristina, who was the sister of Edgar the Atheling (great-nephew of Edward the Confessor and last male member of the Saxon royal family). Cristina also had a sister called Margaret who married King Malcolm of Scotland in 1070 (and was eventually canonised as Saint Margaret of Scotland).

The fact that she was the unmarried sister-in-law of the King of Scotland, who had sworn allegiance to William I in 1073, and was possibly in need of provision and protection may explain Cristina's lordship. However, Cristina became a nun late in 1086 and eventually became abbess of Ramsey Abbey near Peterborough.

Longdon had a probable population of about fifty[2] and was held by Turchil of Warwick, a Saxon who held 67 manors in Warwickshire at that time. Turchil had appointed another Saxon, Almar, as a sub-tenant at Longdon.

Ulverlei contained the large moated earthwork known as Hobs Moat which is situated to the west of Hobs Moat Road near Solihull Ice Rink. Many historians have assumed that this was the site of the manor of Ulverlei. William Dugdale,[3] writing in 1656, said:

> I found a large Moat, containing at least an Acre, whereon they say a Castle long since was situate, though now nothing be left thereof ... which tradition hath the more colour of truth, forasmuch as there is a lane, near at hand, bearing the name of Castle lane. Some of the neighbourhood do call this Hoggs moat, which I conceive is intended Ogingsells moat, but by corrupt pronunciation now so termed; for I have seen the name of Odingsells very antiently written Hoginsells.

It was not until 1985 that this theory could be tested by means of archaeology and the partial excavation undertaken between 1985-8 appeared

4 Manor House Farm, Olton, *c.*1910.

to disprove it. Radiocarbon dating and pottery sherds indicated a probable date in the 12th century, which would be too late for the original site of Ulverlei. This date would, however, place the construction of the moated site in the period when the de Limesi or de Oddingsell families held the manor.

A possible site for the manor is in modern Olton, which is thought to mean 'Old Town', almost completely abandoned after the 'new town' of Solihull was created. Place-name evidence exists in Ulverley Green Road and the Ulleries, and as late as 1839 four large fields west of Richmond Road were named Lower, Upper, Middle and Far Wolvey. In addition, Victor Skipp[4] has observed that the main clue to siting an Anglo-Saxon settlement was the positioning of the manor's open fields and that, although it was now impossible to determine exactly where the open fields in Ulverlei were located, it was likely that villeins occupied land in the western part of the manor, possibly near the site of St Margaret's

church (which was founded in the late 19th century).

Finally, there was a timber-framed house known as Manor House Farm (sometimes called Ulverley Hall Farm) near the junction of Castle Lane and Ulverley Green Road until at least 1920, although most of the moat was filled in long before. Bearing in mind the evidence from place names and the fact that this site was near one end of Castle Lane, perhaps this was the site of the original manor, replaced later by a 'modern' status symbol by the Oddingsells farther along the lane.

The new town of Solihull was a creation of the de Limesi family, Norman lords of the manor of Ulverlei in the 12th century. The site was chosen because it lay at the crossing of two important trade routes at the eastern edge of the manor, near its boundary with neighbouring Longdon. One route originated in Worcester and passed through Droitwich (important even before the Roman invasion for its salt), terminating at Coventry, which was an extremely important

5 King Henry III (based on his effigy in Westminster Abbey) with a knight and his lady in the 13th century.

6 Church Hill, Solihull, 1909.

trading centre in the early Middle Ages. The second route linked Warwick and Birmingham, which both had markets and fairs. Merchants and traders frequented both routes and would provide custom for the proposed market at Solihull.

Solihull is situated at the top of a steep hill which gives the town its name, derived from the Anglo Saxon 'muddy or miry hill'. It also acquired the nickname 'Pigstye hill'. The name 'Solyhull' first appears in the 'Red Book of the Exchequer', a tax list dating from around 1170. The name sounds like a cry from the heart of the original residents—the mud was a result of the soil composition of red clay which would make the hill difficult to ascend in wet weather. The steep slope of Church Hill Road was still causing haulage problems in the late 19th century when extra horses would be used to help drag heavy carts to the top.

The town flourished at first and was so successful by 1242 that Henry III granted a charter to William de Oddingsell (a descendant of the de Limesi) who was then lord of the manor. The charter permitted a weekly market and an annual three-day fair held on the feast day of the town's patron saint, Alphege. Eventually, the success of the market declined and the town dwindled into little more than a village in a remote part of Warwickshire, surrounded by country lanes and farmland.

7 Blossomfield Road, Solihull, *c.*1900.

Delightful descriptions of the village in the early 19th century have been recorded by Irving van Wart,[5] nephew of Washington Irving the American author. Irving van Wart was born in New York around 1808 and was taken as a young child to Birmingham where his father became a successful merchant. The family were frequently visited by their famous literary relation. Irving was sent to a private boarding school in Solihull and still remembered the 'ancient village in a rural section of the rich county of Warwick' more than sixty years later when he published his autobiography (when he was again a resident of Birmingham).

He described Church Hill as a 'rural lane of steep descent, bordered by high hedges, and, at intervals, overshadowed by lofty trees, … and

traversing a brook, winds away amid rich meadowland, refreshed by rivulets, intersected by green gipsy-lanes, and variegated by numerous woods.'

Almost fifty years later Geoffrey Martineau, who was born in Solihull in 1863, recorded some of his personal memories[6] of the village. He mentioned country lanes bordered by deep ditches, as in Lode Lane where he remembered his Aunt Caroline slipping into a ditch one evening in the dark as she went out to dinner with his parents. The unfortunate Caroline found that the ditch was full of snow and water and was forced to return home to change her clothes. Mr. Martineau remembered another occasion when his nursemaid fell into one of the ditches in Lode Lane up to her waist—this became known by the entire household as 'Nannie's Ditch'.

8   Malvern Park Farm, Solihull, 1892.

At first most farming on the medieval manors would have been carried out in open fields used in common by the villagers. However individuals were later allowed to create their own farmsteads in the unused land known as the foreign within the manor. Eventually many moated sites were established in the area and may indicate individual inclosures of land or assarts as more land was cleared in the woodland and allocated to families. Some of these survive today, usually without their moats, but 15th-century Berry Hall in Ravenshaw Lane has retained part of its moat although the house has been reduced in size.

By the 16th century about two-thirds of the local farmland was used as pasture with the remaining third used for growing crops such as wheat, rye and oats and occasionally peas, plus a small amount of flax and hemp from the mid-17th century onwards.

Two centuries later the balance had changed and arable farming occupied two-thirds of the farmland. By this time farmers routinely used systems of crop rotation to farm the land effectively. In 1794 John Wedge (who was the agent for the Earl of Aylesford at nearby Packington) noted[7] more than 25 systems of rotation in use in the county, many of them variations on the 'Norfolk' system. Many of these systems were very complex and some took as long as 15 years to work through the cycle.

Tithe surveys were carried out in 1789 and 1840 which provide some information about farms in the parish and some examples follow. Blossomfield Farm in Blossomfield Road was one of the oldest farms in the parish, taking its name from the Flemish Blosmevile family who were first recorded in the late 13th century. By 1789 it was owned by the Wigley family and rented to

Samuel Chambers who was growing a large amount of corn but in 1840 the tenant was John Doughty, who used most fields as grassland, presumably for grazing.

Broad Oaks Farm was a fairly small farm with fields extending to the north of Warwick Road at World's End. George Bannister owned the farm in 1789 and farmed there himself, growing grass, wheat and barley (possibly as cash crops). In 1840 the farm was owned by John Gough and rented to John Addison who was growing arable crops. Broad Oaks farmhouse survives at the corner of Buryfield Road but its farmland is now St Helen's Road.

Copt Heath Farm was let to Joseph Cattell by Lord Wentworth, the owner in 1789, and the farm was a stock farm with herds of sheep and cattle and about two-thirds of the land used for grazing. Lady Byron (wife of the poet) owned the farm in 1840 and rented it to John Cattell.

9 (*Left*) Mrs. Warner on the right with daughter Winnie on the left and friend harvesting in Lugtrout Lane.

10 (*Below*) Mrs. Warner feeding piglets.

The farm had been enlarged by about twelve acres and now had more arable land.

There were over fifty farms in the parish by the mid-19th century and a number of smallholdings, such as that held by the Warner family in Lugtrout Lane. Many of the farmhouses such as Silhill Hall, Hillfield Hall and Longdon Hall Farm had formerly been halls or houses occupied by the gentry but had changed use over the years.

Many of the houses were timber-framed and dated from the 16th and 17th centuries and some had been surrounded by moats. Malvern Park Farm in Widney Manor Road was built in the 16th century. Sometimes known as Witley Farm, the Grade II* listed timber-framed house survives today, although its farmland has now disappeared. The moat at Moat Farm to the east of Lode Lane survived until at least the end of the 19th century. The Council depot in Moat Lane later occupied the site.

11 Mrs. Warner near haystack, Lugtrout Lane.

12 John Markham at Whar Hall Farm, Damson Lane, c.1890.

As late as 1940 *Kelly's Directory* stated that the soil in the area was predominantly sand and gravel with a loamy sub-soil. Wheat, oats and barley were listed as the main crops. Many farms survived in the Solihull area in the mid-20th century and most were described as 'mixed' farms or dairy farms.

The Elmdon Hall Estate owned a number of farms which were sold as separate items in two sales disposing of the estate in 1920 and 1930. Tanhouse Farm was located in Old Lode Lane and was rented to Francis Symes in 1920 when its 153 acres were used for arable crops and as grazing for a dairy herd. The house was timber-framed but covered in stucco and had originally been moated. It took its name from a tanyard once operating there. The house was demolished after the Second World War when the Tanhouse Farm Road estate was built on its fields.

13   (*Left*) Bill Markham at Whar Hall Farm, 1930s.

14   (*Below*) Farming at Malvern Park Farm, Widney Manor Road.

15   Harvesting in St Bernard's Road, *c.*1880.

16   Foredrove Farm, 1920.

17 Dovehouse Farm, *c*.1930.

18 George Beck from Malvern Park Farm, 1920s.

19 H. Morgan, Manor Farm.

Foredrove Farm in Damson Lane was descibed as a mixed farm in 1920 when G.W. Franklin was the tenant farmer and, like Rowood Farm near Lode Lane, was destined to become a housing estate in the post Second World War period. Ironically, Foredrove Farm was described in the Elmdon Estate Sale Catalogue as 'one of the best farms on the estate. The house and buildings are of a superior character and excellently placed for economic working'. The catalogue noted for Rowood Farm that it was within easy distance of Solihull, 'where there is a large and increasing population and a ready market for all farm produce'.

Other farms owned by the Estate and sold in 1920 were Manor House Farm at Olton, Dovehouse Farm near Olton, Olton Farm, Odensil Farm and Dunstan Farm at Elmdon. Whar Hall and Village Farms at Elmdon were included in the 1930 sale when Elmdon Hall was also sold. Whar Hall eventually became a housing estate but Village Farm survives on the south side of the Coventry Road.

Shelly Farm was possibly the last working farm in the vicinity of Solihull town. This farm did not cease its activities until *c.*1985 when its fields became part of the Cranmore-Widney development. The farmhouse, which is a Grade II listed building, survives (unlike so many others in the locality) but is now a public house with a family restaurant housed in the former barn. Two 18th-century farmhouses are also incorporated in the development—Libbards House and Hillfield Farm have been converted for housing, keeping many of their original features.

Two

Trade and Industry

It was noted in the first chapter that the town of Solihull was created by the de Limesi family in the 12th century. The site was chosen for its commercial potential at the crossing of two trade routes and was also important for its proximity to the neighbouring manor of Longdon with the possibility of utilising resources there.

There is evidence to suggest that the town was laid out with a grid of streets containing plots of land available for rent to attract crafts-men and traders to settle here. These burgage plots were rented by free men called burgesses who owed no labour service to the lord of the manor, unlike the villeins who were obliged to work for their lord in return for their allowance of a share in the common land to grow crops for their own use. Burgesses were often craftsmen and each plot would provide sufficient space for a workshop, a shop and living accommodation for the family, with possibly a little land to grow vegetables.

The weekly market and annual fair allowed by the charter of 1242 was intended to attract itinerant traders travelling between larger com-mercial centres. Some would be pedlars with a back pack containing their wares while others

20 The *Saddlers Arms* and (in distance) *Barley Mow*, pre-1899.

would be wealthy merchants with one or more packhorses carrying their goods. Wagons were rarely used because of the difficulty in taking wheeled vehicles over unmade roads which were often muddy or even flooded.

The town prospered in the 13th and early 14th centuries but by the end of the 14th century began to experience a steady decline in importance. Several factors contributed to this decline: after the Oddingsell family died out there was no resident lord of the manor to encourage expansion; the high death rate caused by plagues and epidemics reduced the number of available craftsmen and made people reluctant to visit crowded places such as markets; economic crises followed poor harvests and eventually there was too much competition from neighbouring towns. Solihull was not alone in this experience—in Warwickshire the towns in the agricultural Feldon flourished while those in the Arden declined.

By the early 19th century Solihull was little more than a village in a quiet corner of Warwickshire. Irving van Wart arrived in the village on the coach from Birmingham and later recorded a vivid image in his autobiography:[1]

> The London coaches of old drove past on their daily route, and drew up at the *Barley Mow*, a rustic tavern that marks the entrance to the village. ... Such was the chief intercourse of this secluded village with the ever-changing world. ... Leaving the *Barley Mow* you ascend the main street, margined by trees and old fashioned houses. Grass sprouts from between the rough paving stones, and adds to the air of quiet seclusion which impresses you as you advance.

The earliest known illustration of Solihull is a print produced by Radclyffe and published in a directory in 1829. It shows the High Street with van Wart's 'old fashioned houses'. *Pigot's Directory* dated 1828 described Solihull as 'a small market town ... situated on the great road from Birmingham to Warwick, and consists of one good street, whose houses are neat and disposed on each side of the road.' *Pigot* also recorded a weekly market 'which has dwindled into insignificance' and an annual fair for cattle and

21 High Street by T. Radclyffe, 1829.

22   High Street, 1853.

sheep, still held on 29 April (the transferred date for St Alphege's feast day).

Just over thirty shops and businesses were listed by *Pigot* in 1828 with families provisioned by four butchers, a 'druggist & grocer', a baker, a tallow chandler and three general shopkeepers. Clothing was catered for by three tailors, two boot and shoe makers and a milliner. Other listed trades included a sadler, a blacksmith, a wheelwright, a tanner, a brazier, and a timber merchant and builder. Three attorneys and four surgeons were the only professions listed. Several coaching inns were listed and the *Barley Mow* was particularly important as a stopping place for coaches to London, Leamington and Warwick.

The population of Solihull parish (which still included Shirley, Solihull Lodge and part of Olton) was recorded as 2,878 in 1831 and had a slight increase to 3,333 in 1841. *Pigot's Directory* of 1842 shows little difference in the businesses represented, with just over forty. Trades listed in 1828 were still present and in addition two 'chymists & druggists', a corn dealer and three carpenters were

listed. Auctioneers had joined the attorneys and surgeons in the section for the professions.

Wealthier local residents also shopped farther afield. In October 1838 Rev Archer Clive, Rector of Solihull 1829-47, wrote[2] to his friend Caroline Wigley who was visiting London : 'Pray buy the carpet-rug … and I will honestly pay you when we meet. Will you also be kind enough to buy a box of eau de Cologne at Atkinson's in Bond Street and let it be sent here to me by the coach.'

The following year Archer spent time with his father in London and Caroline (who lived at Olton Hall in Lode Lane) wrote to request that he buy her a gown, change a hat for a larger size and order some books. Archer replied, 'I will order your hat … I have got you Balzac and a very ugly gown, but that is your fault for letting me choose after the experience you have had of my taste.' After a lengthy friendship Archer proposed to Caroline in September 1840 and they were married on 10 November.

The couple sometimes used the shops in Birmingham. Caroline recorded in their joint diary on 26 December 1846, 'We drove to Birming-

23 Mann's Curio Shop.

24 High Street, 1897.

25   High Street, *c*.1907.

ham to do some shopping but all the best shops were shut to keep holiday. It had been announced in the papers but we took no heed'.

The inns and hotels continued to benefit from the trade brought by travellers using coaches to and from Birmingham, Warwick and Leamington, calling at the *George*, *Barley Mow* or *Golden Lion*, but coaches no longer departed for London. Local residents bound for the capital now travelled by railway from Hampton-in-Arden.

In 1852 a railway station opened at Solihull on the new Oxford & Birmingham Railway which had started operation in 1850. The railway brought more residents to the town as business and professional men took the opportunity to move their families out of Birmingham to the pleasant surroundings offered in the Solihull area. As the population gradually increased more shops and services were needed in the town.

Growth was gradual at first with the population recorded as 3,277 in 1861, 3,739 in

1871 and 6,150 in 1891. The *Post Office Directory* of 1860 and *White's Directory* of 1874 showed little change in the number of businesses, although *White* presented a rather different picture from earlier descriptions of a sleepy backwater:

> The town principally consists of one long street (High-Street), with another branching off the road to the Market-place. ... The houses in general are modern and well-built, and many of them are large and handsome. The inhabitants are well supplied with water and gas. The air is salubrious, and the surrounding scenery of a pleasing character. ... The market, which was on a Wednesday, has long been discontinued.

In the mid-19th century streets were quiet and the road surface was rough and dirty. Geoffrey Martineau remembered[3] seeing drovers herding cattle along the roads in the village. The herds would contain hundreds of animals and were

26 Silhill House and shops, *c*.1912.

allowed to travel at their own pace, feeding on grass verges along their way and sometimes completely blocking the village streets. Smaller herds were still driven to abattoirs at local butchers in the early 20th century.

The village streets were frequently muddy and women wore wooden pattens to lift their skirts out of the dirt and protect their boots (which were often made of cloth because leather was expensive). The first pavements, made of cobble stones, were laid in the High Street around 1862. A strip of flat paving stones was laid in the centre for pedestrians.

The cobble stones were finally removed in 1931 but fortunately many photographs survive to record them, including Mr. Mann's 'Olde Curio Shoppe' in the building later occupied by the White Cat Café and now the Fat Cat restaurant. Many memories of the cobble stones have been recorded such as Mrs. Stewart's reminiscences[4] of weeding between them in the

'weedy time' with her sister and brothers in the 1890s. The children would be paid one penny for each bucketful of weeds.

As the town expanded it attracted new tradesmen eager to set up in business. William Saxtree was born in Gloucestershire in 1840 but had moved to Solihull by 1874 when his baker's shop was listed in *White's Directory* in 'New Street' (presumably New Road). The shop later moved to Mill Lane where William built a new bakery at the rear. William died in 1891 and was succeeded by his widow Harriet, who had formed a partnership with John Bullivant from Shirley by 1900 when the bakery traded as Saxtree & Bullivant. The premises were bought by Solihull Gas Company *c*.1919 for use as the Gas Showrooms.

By 1896 the population had risen to over 6,150 and the town was now a busier commercial centre with more than eighty shops and businesses listed in *Kelly's Directory*. Shops were now located in Warwick Road, Mill Lane and Drury Lane in

27 High Street, *c*.1910.

28 Lea's grocer's shop, High Street.

29 Bragg's butcher's shop, High Street, 1908.

addition to the High Street but houses continued to occupy plots in all these roads.

Some businesses were well established and were often family concerns, with several generations involved. Richard Lea's grocer's shop was listed by *White* in the High Street in 1874 when it was also an off-licence. A carrier's cart was available to deliver to customers. Mrs. Mary Ann Lea was listed as the grocer in the High Street by 1896 and was still present in 1912 and Walter Lea was also listed in 1896 as a grocer and wine and spirit merchant in Warwick Road.

The Post Office was situated in the High Street from 1828 to 1911. A local oral tradition recorded that a postmistress early in the 19th century had a habit of opening letters and resealing after illicitly reading them—she allegedly boasted that she would never be taken to task as she knew too much about everyone in the village.

Three members of the Pearman family were responsible for the service for a total of 64 years. Although listed by the 1851 census as a 50-year-

old saddler in Warwick Road, William Pearman became postmaster in 1857, succeeding Thomas Harbourn. In 1860 his wife Susannah was listed as postmistress and by 1874 their daughter Ruth had taken over the business.

In 1911 the Post Office moved to Warwick Road, where it remained in a building opposite the *Saddlers' Arms* until the 1940s, when a new Post Office was built in Station Road. Space was limited in these buildings and consequently mail sorting was carried out at Shirley until a large Post Office and Sorting Office was built in Drury Lane in the 1960s as part of the Mell Square development.

The Bragg family were numerous and diversified into many different trades. Thomas Bragg was listed as a builder and carpenter in Drury Lane in 1874 and Bragg Brothers were builders in 1900. Alfred Bragg had a butcher's shop at the end of the High Street opposite Poplar Road by 1908 where there was a small abattoir. Customers' orders were delivered, if desired, by pony and trap. Harvey Bragg was a boot repairer

30   Bourne's Seed Merchants, High Street, 1930s.

31   Warwick Road, *c*.1908.

32 Marshall's ironmonger's shop, Warwick Road, pre-1900.

in Mill Lane by 1916, George Bragg was a plumber in Mill Lane and Walter Bragg was a painter and decorator in New Road by 1921. Members of the family were still in the Solihull area in the year 2000.

The town continued to expand and by 1900 there were nearly eighty businesses listed in *Kelly's Directory*. A greater variety of goods was available with shops such as James Hodgkiss' berlin wool warehouse, Leal's draper's, Frances Cooke's tobacconist's, Edward Hawkes' furniture dealer's and Thomas Edwards' florist's. There was also more competition: there were several butchers, grocers, bakers, stationers and boot makers.

Gradually shops appeared in Mill Lane, Drury Lane and Warwick Road. Among the shops listed by *Kelly's Directory* for 1900 in Warwick Road were Cornelius Eborall's butcher's, Joseph Whittington's grocer's and Joseph Marshall's ironmonger's.

Edward Hobbins set up a shop in Warwick Road which was described as a watch maker's and jeweller's by 1896. Mr. Hobbins made clocks and watches, carried out repairs and

visited houses to wind clocks, cycling to out-lying houses.

Many memories have been recorded of the clockmaker—Mrs. Harriet Saxtree said[5] that he would remove his boots before entering her house and Mrs. Lines remembered that he did not approve of opening the window in a room containing a clock. Edward's son Arthur took over the business eventually, retiring at the age of 84 in the late 1960s (although even then he continued to do occasional repairs 'to keep himself occupied'). The shop remained much as it had been since it was opened in the 19th century, with green wooden shutters and an ancient clock in the window while Arthur worked by the light of an oil lamp.

By 1911 Arthur Hobbins had taken up photography and advertised services such as 'high-class' portraits and sepia prints. When Arthur's shop was demolished in the late 1960s a collection of glass negatives was discovered and saved from destruction. Copies are filed in Solihull Library.

After the First World War more houses were built in the area with many new roads cut through former farmland. Shops were built in Poplar Road

33 Poplar Road, *c.*1930.

in the 1920s on the site formerly occupied by
Silhill House and its gardens, and more shops
appeared in Station Road in the 1930s. 'Chain
stores' such as the Co-operative Stores and
Woolworth's (built on the site of a house called
the Gables formerly occupied by Dr. Bernays)
started to appear in the 1930s, but individual
businesses still predominated.

Many of these have been recorded in the
written memoirs of former residents in which
shopkeepers are fondly remembered. The pace
of life was still slow; shopkeepers took time to
chat to customers and orders were frequently
delivered. Mrs. Gorton, writing in 1988,
remembered[6] walking round to the High Street
from her house in Herbert Road and visiting
Hurrell's Stores to leave her grocery order (later
delivered by a boy on a bicycle with a large
basket). Mrs. Gorton also frequented the butcher's
shop owned by G.M. Hull, who delivered to
customers using a horse and cart, and the greengrocer's shop run by the Blizzard twins.

Those who were children in the 1930s recall
happy hours spent choosing toys in Deebanks'
shop, especially at Christmas time when the shop
was described as a 'treasure house' with the
interior transformed with fairy lights. Others
remember the special ice-creams at Dascombe's
pastrycook's and the eccentricity of the Blizzard
sisters at the greengrocer's.

In the years following the Second World
War there was considerable expansion in the
Solihull area. Many houses were built and the
population continued to increase rapidly. Solihull
was created an Urban District Council in 1932
and the population was then recorded as 25,300
but this increased to 72,000 by 1954 when the
Municipal Borough was formed and rose further
to around 104,000 in 1964. In addition car
ownership increased dramatically in post-war
years—a survey in 1965 revealed a total of over
30,000 vehicles in the area.

In the early 1950s Solihull still retained the
characteristics of a small Warwickshire town. In

1920 probably about a third of the buildings in the High Street were houses and, although most of these had become shops by 1950, the town planners considered that the shopping centre was inadequate to meet the anticipated needs of the second half of the 20th century.

In 1956 Mr. C.R. Hutchinson, the Borough Surveyor, drew up preliminary sketch plans for a new development to replace Mill Lane and Drury Lane, two narrow medieval roads linking High Street and Warwick Road. Solihull Council then approached Norwich Union (who had considerable experience of redeveloping town centres in co-operation with local authorities) and detailed plans were drawn up by the architects Harry Weedon & Partners. Other developers were given the opportunity to submit plans but the Council voted unanimously to proceed with the negotiations with Norwich Union.

Following a public enquiry planning permission was granted by the Ministry of Housing and Local Government in 1962, demolition of the buildings in Mill Lane and Drury Lane began in 1963 and most shops were open by Christmas 1966. The new development was officially opened in May 1967 and named Mell Square in honour of W. Maurice Mell, Town Clerk from 1947 until his sudden death in 1965.

In 1975 the Police Station in Poplar Road was demolished following the completion of the new building in Homer Road, and Poplar Way was built as a covered shopping precinct to link Poplar Road to Mell Square.

Mell Square was refurbished and pedestrianised in 1987-8 and at the same time councillors and town planners once again considered the future of the shopping centre. It was eventually decided to develop the land occupied by the civic centre car park and the Conference & Banqueting Centre. Work began on the Touchwood development in 1999. Touchwood is due to open in September 2001 and will include shops, a multi-screen cinema and restaurants.

The main occupations in the early medieval town would appear to be leather manufacture and working, textiles and metal trades. Skinners, tanners and cordwainers worked in the leather industry and spinning, weaving and dyeing was required for textiles. There is a reference to 'teyntors grene' in the 14th century and

34 Olton Windmill (south side), Lode Lane, 1897.

probably refers to the place where cloth was stretched to dry on tenter hooks. An area of common land at the corner of Drury Lane and Warwick Road was still known as Tainters Green at the end of the 19th century. The High Street was known as 'Le Smythestret' in the 14th century, which indicates a number of blacksmiths, and wire drawers and nail makers were recorded.

In addition to these trades many others were present including potters, coopers, sawyers, carpenters and masons. Mills were an early source of energy and three varieties were developed powered by wind, water and animals. Mill Lane in Solihull was first recorded as 'Myln Lane' in the 15th century but the source of power is not known.

Various windmills have been recorded in the Solihull area including Olton Windmill in Lode Lane, a post-mill in operation until *c.*1878 but left derelict until its demolition around 1900. Windmills were also located in Malvern Park, Copt Heath and Bentley Heath.

35   Henwood Watermill, *c*.1925.

36   Tanyard cottages, Warwick Road, *c*.1930.

37   Solihull Brickworks, Warwick Road (near Brueton Park), *c*.1950.

The nuns at Henwood Priory were granted permission for a watermill on the River Blythe by the 15th century. The present Henwood Mill was built in the 18th century and continued in operation until the 1930s.

The Madeley family owned a tanyard in Warwick Road from at least 1861 until 1867, when Charles Madeley retired. Geoffrey Martineau described[7] the various processes including the lime pits, the tan pits, the engine house with its boiler house and tall chimney stack, the bark shed and the workshops. Mr. Martineau recalled that there was only a low wall between the tan pits and he remembered 'one of my friends falling into a pit one day, and when she was pulled out she was brown all over!'

The bark shed, engine house and chimney were demolished when the tanyard closed but the workshops were converted into cottages. The administrative headquarters of the Church of Jesus Christ of Latter Day Saints now occupies the site of the tanyard cottages. Charles Madeley built a

house called 'Broomfield' on the site of the bark shed.

Several brickyards were located in the area and were sometimes a temporary measure created to provide materials for a specific building because transporting bricks was expensive and time consuming. A brickworks was situated in Warwick Road near the junction with New Road for a time. The first bricks made were used to build Bradford House. Another brickworks occupied the present site of the *Moat House Hotel* in Homer Road for a time around 1900.

Geoffrey Martineau remembered a sawmill and wheelwright's shop in Warwick Road near the *Saddlers Arms* and sheds with sawpits near the junction of the Crescent and Station Road (the owner used water from a nearby brook to flush away the sawdust). A sawmill and timberyard was located in Old Lode Lane in the early 20th century, operated by Frank Dixon from Sheldon.

In 1892 James Wilsdon and Charles George set up a wheelwright and blacksmith's business

38   W. Colley (builders) in former Church House, Drury Lane, *c.*1960.

39   Dixon's timber yard, Old Lode Lane/ Merevale Road, pre-1937.

which was to continue for over a hundred years and become one of the largest companies in Solihull. James Wilsdon was born in Barston in 1866 and learnt his trade from John Findon, a coachbuilder in the village.

George & Wilsdon was located behind a pretty timber-framed cottage in Park Road where James Wilsdon lived with his wife, Amy, and their six children. The business gradually changed emphasis, first manufacturing and selling wagons and then manufacturing commercial vehicle bodies. In about 1912 Mr. George returned to Barston and James Wilsdon took over, trading as Wilsdon & Co and in due course was joined by his sons Walter and Leslie who became partners in the 1920s.

Wilsdon's craftsmen produced vehicles specifically suited to their customers' requirements, gaining a reputation for quality products. By the mid-1930s the company employed 45 people and in 1936 (the year that James Wilsdon retired) the cottage was demolished to make way for a larger factory. The company continued to expand and became market leaders in the production of

40 Commercial vehicle at Wilsdon & Co, Park Road, 1927.

insulated compartments suitable for transporting fish, meat, ice cream and other perishables.

In 1959 Wilsdon & Co Ltd was sold to Allied Bakeries (Associated British Foods) but retained its name and the factory relocated to the Lode Lane industrial estate. Walter and Leslie Wilsdon retired in 1960 and the last link with the family was severed.

Wilsdon's produced a wide range of vehicles throughout the 20th century including motor coaches, fire engines, mobile libraries, coaches for the London Underground and commercial vehicles, especially for the food industry. In 1992 the company proudly celebrated its 100th anniversary but in September 1994 Allied Foods 'reluctantly' decided to close down the Solihull factory because of a decline in demand.

George Lines set up in business in Church Hill as a well-sinker and pump-maker in the late 19th century. Born in Yardley in 1862 George learnt his trade from his uncle, William Powell, and by 1891 had opened a shop in the High Street where his new wife Annie sold a wide variety of household goods. Before water was

41 Water engineering by G. Lines & Sons Ltd.

42   R.G. Boardman Ltd., Lode Lane, *c*.1960.

supplied through water mains most people had their own private well or pump, although some were forced to use communal pumps.

Mr. Lines' business expanded into water engineering in the 20th century, sinking artesian wells and constructing water systems for factories. Two sons, William and Harold, joined their father in the business and William gained a reputation as a water-diviner. George and Annie's youngest child was Charles (1913-2000), who is fondly remembered for his work with the National Trust (for which he was awarded the MBE), his dedication to Solihull Society of Arts and Solihull Manor House Trust, his historical research and many lectures and publications.

In 1939 the Ministry of Defence made agreements with the major motor car manufacturers to produce components for aeroplanes and military vehicles for the duration of the Second World War. Plans were made for 'shadow factories', parallel factories with duplicate production lines so that supply was not interrupted in the event of enemy action. A 'shadow factory' was built in Lode Lane for the Rover company which as the Meteor Works became the main place of production for Rover cars in the post-war years. Land Rover now occupies the site and is one of the largest employers in the Solihull area today.

In the second half of the 20th century industrial estates were created in Lode Lane and Cranmore Boulevard in Shirley in an attempt to bring several small, scattered industrial concerns together. Some of the first companies to move to Lode Lane were R.G. Boardman (producers of specialist tools for the rubber industry), Economic Water Softeners Ltd, Retselp Engineering and Bernard Instone's Langstone Works producing high quality jewellery.

In recent years business parks have been developed at Monkspath and Bickenhill and Solihull Council have encouraged the construction of prestigious office developments in the town centre.

Three

Transport

The earliest method of travelling was on foot and early travellers would have made use of paths and tracks through the local woodland and across the open heathland. Horses, donkeys and mules were later used for individuals to ride, or as pack animals. They were also used to pull vehicles such as carts, wagons, carriages and carriers' carts.

Roads and tracks had no surface covering and would be difficult in wet weather when people and their horses or vehicles could be hampered by mud. Solihull's 'muddy hill', consisting of red clay which becomes stiff and unyielding in wet weather, is a prime local example. Rivers and streams could also cause problems, especially when in flood. Travellers would be forced to plan their routes to take advantage of rare fords and bridges, such as the ford across the River Blythe at

Hampton-in-Arden, with the adjacent packhorse bridge erected in the 15th century, and Sandal's Bridge on the Warwick Road outside Solihull. The packhorse bridge is now a scheduled ancient monument and can be viewed at the end of Marsh Lane.

By the 16th century parishes were responsible for maintaining the roads within their boundaries. There was therefore no consistency in the quality of roads from one parish to the next. During the 18th century turnpike roads, administered by trusts, were introduced to improve the quality of main roads and reduce travelling times for passengers and the mail. The turnpike trusts charged travellers a toll to use the new roads. Communications were improved but the tolls were unpopular, especially for those people travelling short distances in their own

43 Warwick Road, near bridge over River Blythe.

neighbourhood. Local residents sometimes tried to evade payment, often by avoiding passing through the turnpike gate. According to an oral tradition a farmer in Shirley was well known for taking to a field path to avoid the turnpike gate at the *Saracen's Head* on the Stratford Road.

The Warwick Road Turnpike Trust was set up by Act of Parliament in 1825 and made improvements including straightening bends at Olton where the 'Old' Warwick Road still exists. The improved route brought custom to the coaching inns in Solihull such as the *Barley Mow* (originally called the *Limerick Castle*), the *George Hotel* and a large establishment called the *White Swan* at the corner of Poplar Road and Station Road.

Pigot's Directory of 1828 records the *Royal Mail*, *Royal Express* and *Crown Prince* calling daily at the *Barley Mow* en route for London from Birmingham (the first called at the *George* on the return trip). The *Regulator*, the *Telegraph* and the *Amicable* called daily on their journeys to Oxford, and Warwick and Leamington.

Geoffrey Martineau recalled[1] the comments made by his maternal grandmother about changing horses in Solihull during her childhood journeys in the early 19th century between the two family homes in London and North Wales. Sometimes they changed horses at the *George* and then turned into Drury Lane to return to the Warwick Road, passing through the farmyard gates of Touchwood Hall (where Geoffrey lived after his marriage to Jessie Madeley). On other occasions they changed horses at the *Swan* and then rejoined Warwick Road by travelling along Streetsbrook Road to Olton.

Pigot also noted carriers' carts which went to Birmingham three days a week and by 1850 *White's Directory* listed a horse-drawn omnibus service to Birmingham on Mondays, Thursdays and Saturdays at 9.00a.m. (no mention was made of a return journey).

In the 1790s work began on the Warwick and Birmingham Canal which passes to the north of Solihull town on its route between Olton and Knowle. Although the Canal made little difference to the area, its actual construction must have caused considerable impact on the small rural communities there.

44   *George Hotel, c.1863.*

45 Excursion from Solihull, *c*.1900 (the Rev. Harvey Brooks centre front row).

Hundreds of men were required: the labourers or 'navvies' who dug the canal, blacksmiths to shoe the horses and maintain the tools, farriers to look after the horses, puddlers to treat the sides of the canal to prevent water leaking, engineers to supervise the work and cooks to feed everyone. Temporary barracks were erected at the side of the canal to house this workforce. The crew may have remained in the Solihull area for longer than usual because they also had to construct Olton Mere to act as a reservoir for the canal by damming two streams. A reservoir is necessary to replace some of the water lost when boats pass through locks.

The canal opened in 1800 and wharves were established at Knowle and Olton, but it did not bring trade or industry as in other parts of the country. It was to prove useful, however, in 1869 when Solihull Gas Works was constructed alongside so that coal for gas production could be delivered by boat. The canal is now part of the Grand Union Canal.

The first railway in the area was the London & Birmingham Railway which opened in 1838, and passed through Hampton-in-Arden where a railway station was built. This station was used by wealthy families such as the Rev. Archer Clive, Rector of Solihull 1829-47, and his wife Caroline when they wished to travel to London.

In the 1850s a railway came to Solihull and this became the catalyst for much of the future development of the town. The Oxford & Birmingham Railway had a route from Snow Hill Station in Birmingham to Oxford which passed through Solihull. It later merged with the Great Western Railway (GWR). Solihull Station opened in 1852 and gave business and professional men the opportunity of moving to live in a healthy, 'salubrious' atmosphere while commuting to their offices in Birmingham. Stations were also

opened at Dorridge, Widney Manor and Olton and the eventual result in all three settlements was suburbanisation.

The coaching inns soon lost their trade when the railway came. By 1842 the London coaches were no longer in operation and passengers travelled to the capital on the new railway from Hampton-in-Arden. Some inns managed to stay in business but the *Swan* had closed by 1828 and became a private house known as Silhill House. It was the home of the Chattock family for many years and was eventually demolished in the 1920s to make way for a parade of shops.

By the late 19th century many local residents would still have had no alternative to walking for most of their journeys but some would have been able to afford a pony and trap, or a small cart, or a horse to ride while wealthier families maintained a horse and carriage. Accidents were fairly common, especially as the roads were often in poor condition. Caroline Clive recorded in her diary[2] that her pony stumbled and fell to its knees,

46 Warwick & Birmingham Canal near Damson Lane, *c.*1926.

47 Solihull railway station, post-1902.

48 Construction on Great Western Railway at Solihull, 1930s.

49 Bertie Gray and pony, *c.*1880s.

50   Unknown riders.

51   Dr. Edward Sutton Page and carriage in the Square.

receiving a cut over its eye. Fortunately Caroline (who was lame through infantile paralysis) did not lose her seat, although her cousin 'Gumley' Wilson recorded that she had frequent falls.

Charles Burd, the Vicar of Shirley, was not so lucky when he had an accident in Marshall Lake Road, Shirley in 1886. Mr. Burd received head injuries and was not able to work for several months. Major-General Sir James Johnstone, from Fulford Hall, was even more unlucky in June 1895. Johnstone, Chairman of the Governors of Solihull School, was thrown from his horse and was 'so seriously hurt that he never regained consciousness' and died shortly afterwards. A stone was erected to his memory in Fulford Hall Road, marking the location of the accident.

Many incidents had less tragic results, such as the collision recorded by Geoffrey Martineau:[3] 'One of the gentlemen from Berry Hall drove a very fast trotting horse in a dog-cart, and … the occupant of Malvern Hall did the same, and one

52 Unknown lady in pony cart.

day, one of them was driving down to the Station, and the other was driving away from the Station, and … they ran into one another, and the wheels locked and upset both of them and their footmen also. Fortunately, none of them were hurt; and

53 Ledbrook's Great Western Mews with horse-drawn hearse and carriage (outside the Post Office), *c*.1890.

although both were in a fearful rage with each other, they were most polite and asking pardon etc'.

Horse-drawn transport continued into the 20th century. The carriage belonging to Canon H.G. Hayter, Rector of Elmdon, was a common sight in Solihull High Street until 1935 and 'Cabbie' Williams continued to use a horse-drawn carriage as a taxi, refusing to have any dealings with new inventions such as the motor car. He continued to stable his horses at the *Royal Oak Hotel* in the High Street during the 1930s.

The bicycle was introduced in the late 19th century and quickly became very popular. Although very expensive at first, prices soon became more affordable and many more people were able to afford their own transport. Increased leisure time gave people more opportunity to go cycling as a recreational activity and cycling clubs were created. On Sundays and Bank Holidays many cyclists passed through the area from

54   Traffic in the High Street, *c.*1910.

55   Children with bicycles, *c.*1910.

56   Dr. Adolphus Bernays with Joseph Fripp, 1907.

57   Motor accident at junction of Warwick Road and Ashleigh Road, 1914.

58   Motor coach at Wilsdon & Co, Park Road, 1920s.

Birmingham on their travels. Edith Holden, in her nature notes for 1906, published as *Country Diary of an Edwardian Lady*, often records that she cycled from her home in Olton to places such as Packwood or Elmdon in search of nature specimens and views to sketch.

The motor car became available at the end of the 19th century. At first only a luxury item for the extremely rich, it gradually came within the reach of the middle classes. One of the earliest

motorists in Solihull was Dr. Adolphus Bernays who had several different vehicles and employed a chauffeur called Joseph Fripp.

Motor vehicles caused problems almost immediately. By June 1903 Solihull Rural District Council (RDC) was concerned by the amount of dust caused by traffic. The RDC considered that the dust damaged crops and was dangerous to pedestrians because it limited their vision. The Council was also concerned about damage to highways and the consequent increased expense of maintenance and the safety hazard to other road users, especially in respect of the speed of motor vehicles. By 1905 the RDC claimed that there were 'daily' reports of accidents and in 1907 proposed to introduce a speed limit of eight miles per hour through towns and villages. Pollution caused by emissions from motor vehicles was recognised as a public health problem by 1907.

The increase in the number of motor vehicles led to the demand for motor garages to supply the necessary fuel and assist with maintenance. Garages opened in Solihull and Shirley, the latter being described by Noel Boston[4] in 1929 as 'the village of petrol pumps'.

A public bus service through Solihull was in operation by the 1930s, operated by the Midland Red company.

59   Rogers' Garage, Warwick Road.

Four

Religion

Domesday Book records a priest at Ulverlei so there was probably a church or chapel in existence by 1086, although nothing further is known.

Solihull Church was founded sometime during the 12th century, following the creation of the market town by the de Limesi family. The church is dedicated to St Alphege who was Archbishop of Canterbury from 1005 until his martyrdom by the Danes at Greenwich in 1012.

The original building would have been smaller than the present church, with a low square tower typical of the Norman period. Philip Martineau was a historian who lived in Solihull at the beginning of the 20th century. Martineau wrote the scholarly introduction to Robert Pemberton's book *Solihull and its Church*, published in 1905, and he also made a drawing of the probable appearance of the original building.

The new town of Solihull flourished and became increasingly prosperous after William de Oddingsell was granted his market charter in 1242. William was succeeded as lord of the manor of Ulverlei by his son. William de Oddingsell junior was a wealthy man who married well—his wife was Ela, daughter of the Earl of Salisbury and great-granddaughter of Henry II and his mistress, Fair Rosamund. William was knighted in 1283 and as early as the 1270s started to enlarge and rebuild the church.

St. Alphege Church, Solihull. Probable aspect c. 1240.
N.B.—Chancel in outline only as none of the original structure exists.

After P. E. MARTINEAU.

60 St Alphege Church: possible appearance, *c*.1240 (after P. Martineau).

Sir William died in 1295 but the work of rebuilding the church continued, although the pace was slower. The chancel and chantry chapels were completed by about 1277; then the south transept, north transept and north aisle and porch were added in the 14th century. The upper part of the tower and the spire were built in the 15th century and finally the nave and south aisle were completed by 1535. The result is a large, beautiful building which has been an important landmark in the town ever since and to this day provides a focal point for the centre of Solihull. Several restorations and repairs have been necessary, notably in 1757 after the collapse of the original spire and in 1879 when the building was closed for 18 months. In 1929 work was started to strengthen the wall in the south aisle, because pressure from the roof was causing the wall to move outwards. Large timber supports were used inside and out until stone buttresses were built in 1953. An extension was added in 1985 to provide a new vestry and toilet facilities and was officially opened by HRH Princess Margaret.

Solihull parish was large and its population was widely dispersed. In 1831 the Rev. Archer Clive, Rector of Solihull 1829-47, built a chapel-of-ease in Stratford Road (about two miles from Solihull) in response to a petition from Shirley residents. The land was donated by Archer's

61   St Alphege Church from the east, *c*.1900.

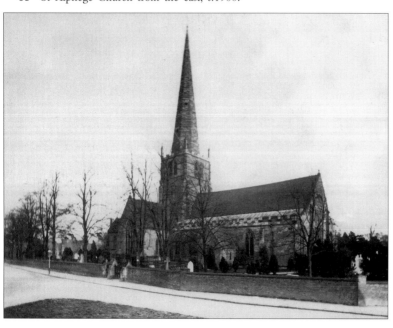

62   St Alphege Church from the Square, pre-1921.

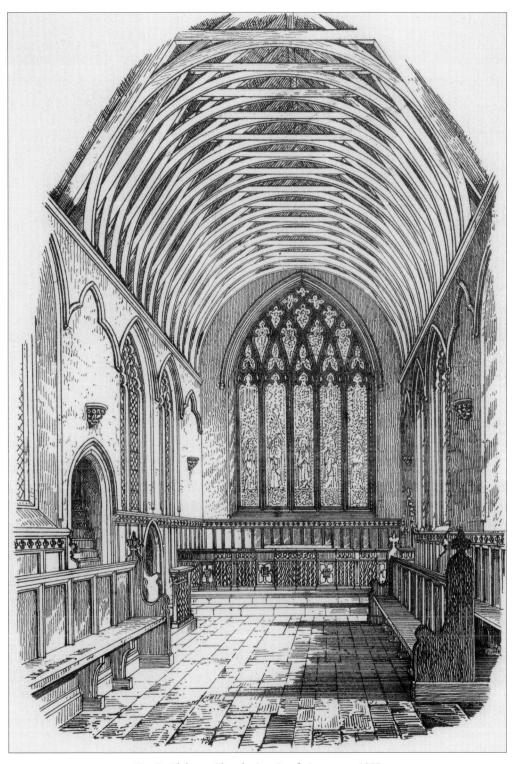

63   St Alphege Church, interior facing east, *c*.1858.

64 St Alphege Church, interior facing west.

cousin, the Earl of Plymouth, and the chapel was consecrated by the Bishop of Lichfield on 2 August 1832. The chapel was dedicated to St James and became Shirley parish church when a new parish was created in 1843.

In the second half of the 19th century the population began to increase as a result of improved transport, especially after the Oxford & Birmingham Railway opened in 1850, attracting commuters from Birmingham. To assist parishioners and help attract new churchgoers a mission church was established at Bentley Heath in 1870 in a new purpose-built dual-use school and church in Widney Road (formerly known as Rotton Row). George Homer, of Station Road, Solihull, left £500 when he died in 1867 to build a school and the land was given by the Rev. John Holbeche Short of Temple Balsall.

On 1 May 1940 Bentley Heath was transferred from Solihull parish to Dorridge, which then became a separate parish. The change had been suggested earlier by the diocesan authorities but the Rector, the Rev. Edward Fraser, had taken four years to 'allow sufficient time to really ponder the problem'.[1] The Mission Church was renamed St James Church c.1956 and closed in

1975, reopening in the new Bentley Heath School in 1982.

Catherine-de-Barnes Mission Church was built by Joseph Gillott of Berry Hall in 1879 for use as a school during the week and as a church on Sundays. Still part of Solihull parish, it was in effect a chapel-of-ease to St Alphege Church and was usually in the care of one of the curates. The church was officially opened by the Bishop of Worcester on 27 October 1879 and was renamed St Catherine's Church on 24 November 1963. Joseph Gillott's wife, Maria, died in 1881 and in her memory he commissioned a stained glass window for the chancel. It was designed by a member of the Pippet family from Solihull and made by Hardman of Birmingham.

The population of Solihull increased dramatically during the mid-20th century. As a consequence of new housing developments in the parish, district churches were created to provide local centres of worship for emerging communities and to provide extra accommodation.

Housing developments in the Elmdon Heath area in the 1930s prompted the Rector of Solihull, the Rev. C.O.R. Wormald, to propose the establishment of a mission church in 1935. A plot of land in Cornyx Lane was donated by the Rev. R.H. Couchman and plans for a dual-purpose church and community centre were drawn up by Leslie Moore, consultant architect to St Alphege Church. The foundation stone was laid by Captain Oliver Bird on 23 September 1939 but the building work (by Bragg Brothers of Solihull) was delayed by the Second World War and it was 1950 before the building was completed and dedicated to St Francis of Assisi.

By 1952 many new houses had been built in the Hobs Moat area and more were planned. As this was about three miles from St Alphege Church it was proposed to build a daughter church to cater for the spiritual needs of the new residents. In Spring 1952 the Rector, the Rev. Edward Fraser, estimated that the new church would need to serve at least 15,000 people. The Rev. E.A. Cooke was appointed priest-in-charge in 1954 and services were held first in the Scout Hut in Brackley's Way and from Easter 1955 in

65 The Rev. T.B. Harvey Brooks, Rector of Solihull, 1894-1926.

66 St Alphege Church Choir, *c.*1903.

67 St Augustine's Church, pre-1904.

Ulverley School Hall. Plans were drawn up by the architect Mr. Leslie Moore for a church hall and vicarage on a site already acquired, and the hall was opened in 1956. A church was designed by the architect Laurence King. The foundation stone was laid in July 1966 and the church, dedicated to St Mary, opened in 1967. St Mary's Church later became a separate parish.

Houses were also built in the Buryfield Road area in the 1950s and St Helen's Fellowship was founded after a Solihull Parish Mission in 1958. Initially a fellowship meeting and Sunday School held in private houses, it later transferred to a school. In 1961 the Rev. R.H. Couchman donated a plot of land in St Helen's Road and temporary huts were erected. St Helen's Church Centre was finally completed in 1975 and is also a dual-purpose building.

The Cheltondale Road estate was also developed in the early 1950s and Sunday school classes were started in houses to help families with small children (many of whom had no private transport). The 1958 Parish Mission proposed the creation of a Sunday School in Sharmans Cross Junior School and this was followed by regular Sunday Eucharist services in 1965. A house in Cheltondale Road was purchased in 1976 for the use of a curate and a chapel was added in 1979 when St Michael's District Church was created. Oak Cottage in Bryanston Road was bought in 1992 to replace the Cheltondale Road house and was converted for use as a team vicarage and church centre with meeting rooms.

A priory for Benedictine nuns was founded at Henwood near Catherine-de-Barnes sometime between 1154 and 1189 by Ketelberne, Lord of the Manor of Longdon. The priory was dedicated to St Margaret of Antioch and appears to have been quite small—by 1404 only 12 nuns were recorded. It was closed by the Commissioners of Henry VIII at the time of the Dissolution of monasteries. At that time there was only the prioress, Joan Higford or Hugford, and six nuns. Several dependents, including a priest and lay servants, were recorded but the buildings were described as ruinous and decayed. Joan was given a pension of £3 6s. 8d. a year and there is a local tradition that she and her sisters were sheltered for a time at the house afterwards known as the 'Priory' at the top of Church Hill opposite St Alphege Church. Henwood Priory was purchased by John Hugford (possibly a relative of the last prioress).

Hugford demolished the priory church and converted other buildings into a house which remained in his family until around 1636. The house survived until 1824 when the then owner, Jacob Wise, pulled it down and built a new house nearby. Henwood Hall is now a Grade II listed building. Local traditions state that Jacob's fiancee refused to live in the house because it was haunted (or because it had formerly been a religious house). Fragments of stone from the old house, including carvings, were used in the garden wall of the new house and wooden panelling was transferred to Solihull Rectory and Olton Hall in Lode Lane. Sadly, both buildings were demolished in the 1930s and it is not known if the panelling survived.

John Howman, known as John de Feckenham, was Rector of Solihull at the time of the Reformation and refused to accept the new liturgy. He was imprisoned in the Tower of London during the reign of Edward VI but released when Mary I came to the throne. He was appointed Abbot of the revived monastery of Westminster and also made chaplain and confessor to the Queen. When Elizabeth I became Queen, de Feckenham again refused to accept the new liturgy, in spite of allegedly being offered the vacant post of Archbishop of Canterbury if he would recant, and died in 1585 after many years' imprisonment in Wisbech Castle.

After the Reformation some local residents would have adhered to the old faith but it was not possible for them to worship openly for many years. It was not until 1778 that the Catholic Relief Act was passed, which abolished the penalty of perpetual imprisonment for Roman Catholic priests and schoolteachers. However there is evidence in the archives of the Franciscan order that a mission existed at Solihull from around 1750 and a gift of land for a church and presbytery was given by Hugford Hassall (who lived at the 'Priory') in 1760. The first Roman Catholic priest, John Waring, was appointed in 1776 and a painting shows the 'Old Presbytery', presumably built on the land given by Hugford Hassall.

A chapel was also built on the land given by Hassall but no illustration or description survives. Bernard Malley, writing in *Solihull and the Catholic Faith* published in 1939, commented that it was probably in a position behind the presbytery so that it was less visible from the lane (now Station Road) and would have been a plain and simple building. It is important to remember that there had been much anti-Catholic demonstration in England in the 18th century and the church authorities did not wish to draw undue attention to the building. This chapel was demolished to make room for a new church designed by the architect Augustus Welby Northmore Pugin, who became one of the best known architects of the 19th-century Gothic revival. The church was dedicated to St Augustine of England and was officially opened on 6 February 1839. It was probably the second church designed by Pugin, who took part in the opening ceremony by acting as cross bearer in the procession.

The building was very simple, with an open bell turret and three lancet windows over the entrance. The church was altered several times during the 19th century and changes included the addition of a chancel, a new round bell turret and a single larger window over the entrance. Stained glass windows and other decorations were added, some designed by Joseph Pippet and his sons Oswald, Gabriel and Elphege, who all lived in Solihull.

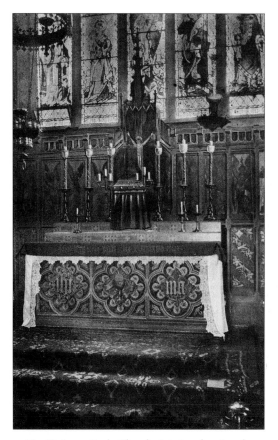

68 St Augustine's Church, interior showing the High Altar, *c*.1914.

St Augustine's Church was considerably enlarged in 1979 but Pugin's church remains as a separate side chapel. According to the *Shell Book of Firsts* St Augustine's was the location of the first wedding in England where the bride and groom left in a motor car. The event took place on 21 April 1897 when Irma L'Hollier married Albert Day. The bride's father, Leon, was Director of the Anglo-French Motor Carriage Co and the bridegroom's father, Edward, was Assistant Manager. *Autocar* magazine reported, 'At the conclusion of the ceremony the wedding party adjourned to the house of the bride's father, where autocars were used in the diversion of the company'.

Protestant Dissenters began to organise Independent worship at Solihull in 1825 when two cottages in Drury Lane were bought to be used as meeting place. The meeting owed its

69   Members of St Augustine's Church.

70   Bethesda Chapel, Union Road.

creation to the Rev John Sibree from Coventry who visited Solihull in 1823 to check its moral and spiritual condition. At the time Charles Curtis was Rector of Solihull but was more interested in hunting and politics than in the spiritual welfare of his parishes (he was also Rector of Birmingham, although he lived at Solihull Rectory).

Solihull was therefore judged to be a 'moral wilderness' in need of spiritual guidance and the Rev. William Hood was appointed as the first Independent minister. With the help of the Independent Chapel in Carrs Lane, Birmingham, Hood managed to build a chapel by 1826. The Bethesda Meeting House was built on a small plot of land in Union Road and the first meeting was held on 9 November 1826, when the church consisted of six members.

William Hood was an enthusiastic and zealous minister and by 1834 his church had almost forty members plus three lay preachers and 16 Sunday School teachers. By 1883 the chapel in Union Road was too small and there was inadequate accommodation for the Sunday School. A new church was built on land at the corner of Drury

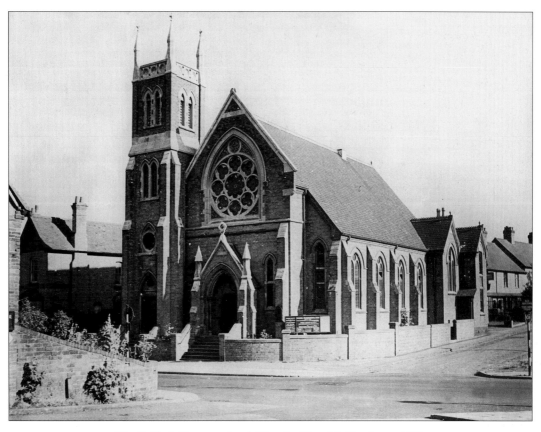

71 Solihull Congregational Church, Warwick Road, pre-1965.

Lane and Warwick Road purchased from Mr. Charles Madeley. The new Congregational Church was built in the 'English Gothic' style at a cost of £2,671, which included making alterations to the old chapel for it to be used as a Sunday School. The opening service was held on 4 March 1884 and the building was to remain in use until 1965 when a new church was built on the opposite side of Warwick Road and the Gothic building was demolished as the road was widened.

In 1974 the Congregational Church in England and Wales united with the Presbyterian Church of England to become the United Reformed Church. At that time the former Congregational Church was given the name Christ Church.

Presbyterian worship began in Solihull in 1946 as a result of lobbying by Mrs. Hilda Alexander, a Presbyterian who had moved to Solihull during the Second World War and then found it difficult to travel to a Presbyterian Church. Services were held in various places including Solihull Council House, Poplar Road, Eversfield School, and Mrs. Alexander's home in Streetsbrook Road until 1950 when a room in the Manor House, Solihull High Street became available.

By 1951 occasional services were held jointly with Solihull Congregational Church and a Presbyterian church was eventually built on a site at the corner of Lode Lane and Hermitage Road. The church had taken several years to complete and opened in 1961. It was dedicated to St Ninian and joined the United Reformed Church in 1974.

The formal history of Methodist worship in Solihull dates from 1883 when Wesleyan Methodist Sunday services were held in the Public Hall in Poplar Road in a room rented for six shillings a week. Before this date it is likely that, from the second half of the 18th century onwards, itinerant preachers visited the area, often preaching

72   Original Methodist Chapel, Blossomfield Road, 1982.

73   Solihull Methodist Church, Blossomfield Road, 1983.

74   Gospel Hall, Poplar Road, 1982.

at open-air meetings. For a brief period between 1842 and 1846 Methodist services were held at a private house but were discontinued due to lack of support.

The Beamond family at Blossomfield Farm were extremely influential in establishing a Methodist presence in the village. John Beamond was called 'the Father of Solihull Wesleyan Methodism' and weekday services were held at his house to supplement the Sunday services (which also transferred to the farm from 1885-9 when numbers decreased). This proved to be a temporary setback and by 1889 the congregation on Sundays merited a return to the Public Hall.

A plot of land at the junction of Streetsbrook Road and Station Road was purchased for £350 in 1903 and the first Methodist Chapel opened there on 15 February 1905. The building was designed by Edwin Shipley and seated 150 people. The first Minister, the Rev. R.C. Barratt, was appointed in September 1902.

The land allowed space for a church to be erected next to the chapel and funds for this were being collected by 1928. However, in 1930

the local authority decided that some of this land would be required for road widening. Another site was found nearby at the junction of Blossomfield Road and Station Approach and a new Methodist Church opened there on 5 June 1937. The original school chapel became the church hall until 1961, when a new larger hall was built next to the church and the old chapel was sold. At the time of writing (2001) the building is in use as the Adult Education Centre, but its future is uncertain and demolition is a possibility.

A Gospel Hall had been built in Poplar Road by the 1950s and was relocated to the corner of Lode Lane and Solihull by-pass in the 1990s when the original building was converted for use as a bank. A Christadelphian Church was built around 1970 and Solihull and District Synagogue was erected in Monastery Drive, Olton, in 1977.

The British administrative headquarters of the Church of Jesus Christ of Latter Day Saints (often known as the Mormon Church) is based in Warwick Road, Solihull. A Mormon Church was built in Hampton Lane in 1985.

Five

Education

A free grammar school was founded in Solihull in 1560 initially using money diverted from chantry chapels in St Alphege Church. Chantries were created in the Middle Ages when wealthy individuals or families gave money to build and maintain separate chapels where masses could be said in perpetuity for the repose of the souls of the benefactors. After the Reformation such practices were suppressed and funds were diverted to charitable purposes (often education).

In Solihull the funds from the chapels dedicated to St Katharine and St Mary in the parish church were the first source of income for the free school, followed in 1566 by the income from the Chantry of St Alphege. In time more gifts and legacies were added to the funds which became known as the Solihull Charity Estate and provided revenue for various charitable purposes in the parish. Some of the gifts had been made at much earlier dates, starting from the 14th century. This may have given rise to a tradition that the school was founded in the reign of Richard II (1377-99). The first documented teacher is Edward Pole, who was appointed in

75 Malvern House (home of Solihull Grammar School until 1882), *c.*1900.

76 Solihull School, Warwick Road, post-1882.

1560. In 1574 a lower school was formed to teach younger boys and a second master or 'usher' was appointed to do this.

In 1566 a deed of enfeoffment entrusted the administration of the revenues of the Charity Estate to a body of trustees who became known as the Feoffees. From the earliest days many of the leading families in Solihull had representatives in the Feoffees including the Warings, Hawes, Greswolds and Hugfords. Thomas Dabridgecourt was the first head of the Feoffees.

According to the Parish Bailiff's accounts a 'scholehous' was built (or rebuilt) in 1615 at a cost of £25 11s. 1d. From at least the 18th century the grammar school was sited in Park Road in the building now known as Malvern House. Additions and extensions were made to the house in the 19th century. Geoffrey Martineau[1] recalled his school days at the Grammar School in Park Road, probably in the 1870s, when there was a great rivalry between the boys from the Grammar

School and those from the National School in Park Road, resulting in skirmishes in the conker season and snowball fights in winter.

In 1850 the Feoffees decided to introduce fees for pupils although they reserved some free places for boys from the Elementary School. Changes were made to the administration of the Solihull Charity Estate in 1879, so that most of the income now went to the school and the Feoffees were replaced by a Board of Governors. That year the first Governors decided to build a new school in Warwick Road and commissioned the architect J.A. Chatwin to design a building which was formally opened on 13 June 1882.

During 1912 the Headmaster, the Rev. A.J. Cooper, appears to have deleted the word 'Grammar' from the school's name. In January 1913 this was queried by the Governors and Dr. Cooper replied[2] that he was acting 'in accordance with the modern custom of schools in any status'.

77 Dining Room, Solihull School, *c.*1930.

78 Dormitory, Solihull School, *c.*1930.

79   First Hockey XI, Solihull School, 1946.

The school continued to accept boarders until the 1960s.

Solihull School (which became an independent school in 1945) has continued to expand on the Warwick Road site. A separate chapel was officially opened by Queen Elizabeth II in 1962, designed by the architect Neville White, a former pupil.

Earlier pupils include the poets Richard Jago (1715-81) and William Shenstone (1714-63) who became members of a literary circle initiated by Lady Luxborough at Barrels Hall near Ullenhall. Jago wrote about their experiences at school in his poem *Edge Hill*, published in 1767 as a memorial to Shenstone, as follows:

Hail Solihull! respectful I salute
Thy walls; more awful once! when, from the Sweets
Of festive Freedom, and Domestic Ease,
With throbbing Heart, to the stern Discipline
Of Pedagogue morose I sad return'd.
But tho' no more his Brow severe, nor Dread
Of birchen Spectre awes my riper Age,
A sterner Tyrant rises to my View,
With deadlier Weapon arm'd. Ah! Critic! spare,
O! spare the Muse, who feels her youthful Fears
On thee transfer'd, and trembles at thy Lash.

The 'morose pedagogue' was Rev. John Crompton who did not apparently spare the rod. It was Crompton's departure to become headmaster at Market Bosworth Grammar School that led to the well-documented rejection of the young Samuel Johnson's application to become headmaster in 1735. The minutes record that:

the Feoffees all agree that he is an excellent scholar, and upon that account deserves much better than to be schoolmaster of Solihull. But then he has the character of being a very haughty, ill-natured gent, and that he has such a way of distorting his face (wh [which] though he cannot help) ye gentlemen think it may affect some of the young ladds; for these two reasons he is not approved of.

The grammar school was created to teach boys but a charity school for girls was founded in 1746 following a bequest from Mrs. Martha Palmer. Additional funds came from Mrs. Elizabeth Fisher and a school was built in School Lane. The building survives as a house.

Solihull had its share of dame schools run by women offering elementary education for a fee of three or four pence a week. Geoffrey Martineau

80   Park Road School and St Alphege Church.

also recalled attending at an early age a Dame School in New Road run by three 'old' ladies. His most lasting impression of the teachers was their fear of thunderstorms—he described them closing windows and covering metal objects such as the fire-irons to prevent being struck by lightning.

Dame schools mostly disappeared after the 1870 Education Act which created the first schools to be organised by local authorities—school boards were set up to manage education districts which were expected to open elementary schools if there was no other provision (for example from charity schools).

A free National School was opened in Park Road in 1850 and was at first an elementary school catering only for boys but girls were admitted from 1862, when the building was enlarged. Martha Palmer's School was then incorporated into the Elementary School.

By the end of the 19th century the population of Solihull was increasing rapidly with the result that the Park Road building was overcrowded. A new school was built in Mill Lane on land given by Joseph Gillott of Berry Hall to accommodate the older boys. The infants and girls remained in the original building, which is now occupied by St Alphege Infants' School. Children often walked three or four miles a day to school and were expected to arrive in all weathers.

81   Park Road School—infants, *c*.1930s.

82 Park Road School—girls, *c.*1910.

Many teachers have given loyal service and have been fondly remembered, including Miss E. Lowe who retired as headmistress in 1894 after 30 years and was given a new sewing machine in 'a very beautifully engraved case'. Miss Sarah Bragg was Headmistress of the Infants' School from 22 June 1896 to 31 March 1932 and was presented on her retirement with a beautifully illuminated 'Testimonial' from scholars, old scholars and friends stating, 'We request acceptance of the accompanying small token of our personal regard and deep appreciation of your thirty five years service as Headmistress. We wish you in your retirement health, prosperity and every happiness.' A list of over 450 names was appended. Unfortunately these good wishes were not fulfilled as Miss Bragg died in February 1934, less than two years after retiring.

St Augustine's Roman Catholic School opened in 1885 in Herbert Road next to the Catholic Church. The school catered for children from Catherine-de-Barnes, Elmdon, Knowle, Shirley and Olton in addition to those from Solihull. Miss Mary O'Gorman was appointed as

83 Park Road School—teachers, *c.*1930s.

84   Mill Lane Boys' School, 1960.

85   Mill Lane Boys' School, football team, 1922.

the sole schoolmistress and the school used the Monitor system to assist the teacher (who had all ages from infants to 15-year-olds). The monitors came from the top standard and helped by passing on their own knowledge.

St Augustine's School quickly earned a good reputation and in the early 20th century many non-Catholic parents chose to send their children here instead of to the National School. St Augustine's School moved to a new site in Whitefields Road in 1991 adjacent to St Peter's R.C. Secondary School, which opened in 1966 as Archbishop Glancey School (named in honour of the Rev. Michael Glancey, parish priest at Solihull 1899-1908) and changed its name in 1974.

The 1880 Education Act made school attendance compulsory until the age of ten. The school leaving age was set at 12 in 1899 and raised to 14 in 1918. Balfour's Education Act of 1902 empowered local authorities to provide both elementary and secondary education.

A secondary school was built for boys in Sharmans Cross Road and officially opened on 22 June 1934. In 1940 Mill Lane Boys' School was closed and the remaining pupils were transferred to the school in Park Road. The Mill Lane building was used as a British Restaurant during the Second World War and then became the church hall for St Alphege Parish Church until the Oliver Bird Hall opened in 1962.

Lode Heath School opened on 4 September 1939, which was an unfortunate date as the Second World War was declared the day before and in addition building work was not completed. Only 30 of the anticipated 200 pupils arrived on the first day and had to be sent home until air-raid shelters had been built. At that time education was the responsibility of Warwickshire Education Authority and there was some local opposition to the creation of a new school from residents who considered that there were insufficient pupils to justify the expense.

Solihull High School for Girls was opened in 1931 at Malvern Hall (the former home of the Greswold family). Warwick County Council bought the house for £5,750 and adapted it for use as a school by building a new wing at an

86 Sharmans Cross School, 1934.

87   Solihull High School for Girls at Malvern Hall, *c.*1934.

88   Art Room, Solihull High School for Girls, *c.*1930.

89 Library, Solihull High School for Girls, *c.*1930.

estimated cost of £25,000 for classrooms with the old house used for administration. The first head-mistress was Miss Forster. In 1974 the school became a co-educational comprehensive school and the falling birthrate led to the school's closure in 1989.

The 1944 Education Act required free provision of secondary education by local authorities. Tudor Grange Grammar School opened in 1956. Harold Cartwright Grammar School for Girls opened in 1961 and actually also accommodated boys until Harold Malley School was completed in 1964. These schools merged in 1974 to become a co-educational comprehensive school renamed Alderbrook.

In the last half of the 20th century several new primary schools opened, including Greswolde School in Buryfield Road, Coppice School in Coppice Road and Oak Cottage in Greswolde Road.

There has been a long tradition of private schools in Solihull. John Powell, who had been Usher at the Grammar School, set up his own school around 1780 at the house known as the Priory at the top of Church Hill. The school could take about 150 pupils, most of whom were

90 Assembly Hall and gym, Solihull High School for Girls, *c.*1930.

boarders. Irving van Wart was a boarder at Powell's School around 1820 and recorded[3] fascinating descriptions of his time in Solihull at the 'large school for preparing boys for college or the professions'. Like Geoffrey Martineau a generation later, van Wart's memories of schooldays include tales of rivalry—this time between his fellow pupils and those of the Grammar School. He also recalled the

91 The Old Priory, Church Hill (home of John Powell's School), *c.*1890.

92   Private school in Warwick Road *c.*1910.

unpredictable temper of a master, pranks such as midnight feasts in the dormitory and dancing lessons in the Old Town Hall together with pupils from a nearby ladies' boarding school.

Warwickshire trade directories record several other private schools in the 19th century: Richard Thompson's Boys' Academy and Miss Wakefield's Ladies' School were listed in 1830. Boarding schools by Richard Thompson, James Pickering, Mrs. Sheldon and Whitwell & Harris (for ladies) were noted in 1842 and Ladies' boarding schools by Mary & Sarah Cattell, Howe & Weeks and Ann Maria Johnson appeared in 1862. Elizabeth and Martha Edwards' school in Warwick Road was listed by 1896 and continued until at least 1908 in a house opposite Solihull School. Pupils for these schools came from the emerging middle classes.

A private girls' school was housed in a large Georgian house called 'Southend' in Station Road

at the beginning of the 20th century. In 1908 the Headmistress was Miss Marion Burd whose father and brother were consecutive vicars of Shirley. Mrs. Crook followed Miss Burd as Headmistress, remaining until at least 1928. Edith Holden gave drawing lessons at the school around 1905 while she was compiling her nature notes which were subsequently published as *Country Diary of an Edwardian Lady*.

Other private schools in the 1920-30s included Miss Constance Walmsley's 'Dilholme' in Park Road and 'Delmara' in Lode Lane opposite Solihull Hospital. Ruckleigh School for girls occupied one of the 'End Houses' in the Square *c.*1919-26 when it was in the charge of Miss Kathleen Cartland, a relative of the novelist Barbara Cartland. Ruckleigh is now situated in Lode Lane.

Tree School (whose name symbolised its primary aim of regarding children as growing

93 Eversfield Preparatory School, Warwick Road.

human beings) opened as a preparatory school in a large house in Warwick Road in 1932 with two Principals: Miss G.M. Jones and Miss Terry Short. The school was very progressive and its prospectus stated: 'We seek the means to preserve trust, initiative and spontaneity of expression in the children while they are developing, that they may lead happy and effectual lives.' The three essentials at the core of the school's policy were happiness, activity and freedom. The school relocated to larger premises in Knowle in 1937 in order to develop a senior school and catered for boys from four to nine years and girls from four to seventeen. Fees *c.*1937 were six guineas a term for children under eight rising to eight guineas for girls 8-11 and 10 guineas for the older girls.

St Martin's School for Girls was founded by two friends, Miss Christine Tucker and Miss Zelie Bull, in 1941 and has occupied several buildings

in the town including 'Alice House' in Homer Road and houses in Station Road. For many years the school offered places for boarders, who lived in houses in Alderbrook Road. St Martin's became a Public School in 1963 and now occupies Malvern Hall, having moved in after the comprehensive school closed in 1974, so that the School is able to accommodate all ages from nursery to sixth form at one location.

A preparatory school was located in a barn at Fowgay Hall, Dingle Lane, in the 1930s and Cedarhurst Preparatory School was established in Park Road by 1941—flats of the same name were built on the site in the mid-1970s. Eversfield Preparatory School opened in May 1931 and continues to the present day in Warwick Road. Eversfield originally took boarders and many were the children of foreign missionaries because the school had a strong Evangelical tradition.

Six

Public Service

From the 11th century the manor was responsible for any local administration and the manor court assumed an organisational role. With the decline of the manorial system the parish took on many of these functions and became responsible for providing local services such as road repair, poor relief and the provision of law and order. These secular responsibilities were organised by a governing body called the vestry which was composed of a selection of male rate-payers.

By the late 18th century five men appear to have taken leading roles in the Solihull Vestry, namely: the Rev. Charles Curtis (Rector),

Thomas Harborne, Richard Chattock, John Powell and John Short. The provision of poor relief was a major responsibility for the parish from 1597. The overseers of the poor had the power to levy rates and these could be supplemented by local charities (such as the Solihull Charity Estate) administered by feoffees (or trustees).

The basic concept of poor law was that anyone capable of working must do so and, if anyone was unable to find work, the parish would provide it. In the 18th century parishes began the system of providing a building where people

94 Old Town Hall, The Square, pre-1880.

95 Solihull Rural District Council and Board of Guardians, 1916.

in receipt of poor relief could live and work together. The first such workhouse in Solihull was built in 1742 in Warwick Road, following a decision taken at a public meeting held in 1740.

In 1834 the Poor Law Amendment Act was passed which abolished the old system of poor relief and brought in unions of parishes administered by boards of guardians. This was an attempt to cope with the difficulties resulting from an increasing population and the consequent rise in the cost of providing relief. The Solihull Union was a coalition of parishes from Yardley to Tanworth-in-Arden. A Union Workhouse was built in 1838 in Union Road, Solihull, to accommodate paupers from all the parishes in the union and the original parish workhouse was converted into houses. By 1874 the Workhouse could accommodate 150 inmates. The Board consisted of 20 elected Guardians plus seven *ex officio* members.

In the mid-19th century parishes began to join together to form boards for functions such as highways and public health. An Act of Parliament in 1872 then designated the Boards of Guardians as Rural Sanitary Authorities (RSAs) with responsibility for public health, drainage and sewerage.

The Solihull RSA was created in April 1873 and consisted of 12 members. The Rev. John Howe became the first Chairman. The RSA soon adopted additional powers with authority over construction of new roads and houses, control of common lodging houses and slaughter houses and the removal of nuisances. Edward Orford Smith, a local solicitor, was appointed Clerk of the RSA and George Edwards was appointed Treasurer. William Harris was given the two posts of Inspector of Nuisances and of Surveyor.

It was decided to appoint a Medical Officer of Health jointly with the districts of Warwick, Rugby, Meriden and Milverton and Dr. George Wilson from Leamington Spa was chosen. As each authority paid in proportion to its rateable value, this meant that Solihull was eventually paying a quarter of Dr. Wilson's salary which was clearly unsatisfactory as he lived at Leamington.

Sewerage was to be one of the first important problems requiring attention by the RSA, especially at Yardley which was becoming rapidly suburbanised. Unfortunately the cost of providing an adequate sewerage system for Yardley was very high and funds for the remaining parishes were depleted. In addition land prices were rising because of the demand to build houses for the wealthy families moving out of Birmingham, and several acres were required for a sewerage irrigation system.

Solihull town was also in need of an improved sewerage system. Orford Smith recorded[1] that the town had been sewered with pipe sewers and brick culverts 'at some remote time' and these were in 'fair condition' but unfortunately the system discharged directly into the River Blythe which was causing pollution to water supplies. The RSA managed to construct a sewerage works near Catherine-de-Barnes by the early 1880s. Other matters tackled by the RSA included public health (with an isolation hospital for infectious diseases erected at Olton in 1876), highways and lighting.

The Solihull RSA was replaced by the Solihull Rural District Council (RDC) after the Local Government Act of 1888 created the system of county councils and urban and rural districts. Warwick County Council was founded in 1890 with Solihull RDC following in 1894.

The Solihull RDC consisted of the parishes of Solihull, Elmdon, Barston, Balsall, Knowle, Nuthurst, Packwood, Baddesley Clinton, Tanworth, Bushwood and Lapworth but excluded Yardley (formerly included in the RSA) which had become very urban in character. Yardley, however, remained a member of the Solihull Union which continued to provide poor relief. A parish council for Solihull was also created and the Solihull Vestry ceased to function from this time.

The RDC consisted of 18 councillors, five of whom represented Solihull. Charles Madeley from Solihull became the first Chairman. The new system of local government was more structured and Solihull RDC was no exception. Committees were created with responsibility for functions such as Finance, Sanitary & Public Works and General Purposes. Various appointments were made including Howard Lloyd (Treasurer), Francis Thompson (Clerk), A.E. Currall (Surveyor), and William Harris (Inspector

96 Mr. A.E. Currall, Surveyor, Solihull R.D.C.

of Nuisances). Dr. Wilson continued to act as Medical Officer of Health for Mid Warwickshire. Most officers of the RDC worked from rooms in houses (often their own homes) but the RDC rented a room in the Public Hall for the Clerk. The Council met in the Board Room of the Union Workhouse.

One improvement made by the RDC was the creation of a cemetery in Solihull. Burials originally took place in the churchyard of Solihull Parish Church, followed by burials in Shirley churchyard after 1832 (when St James Church was built as a chapel-of-ease). There was also a very small burial ground at the Bethesda Chapel in Union Road, Solihull.

By the early 20th century the churchyards were inadequate for the expanding area so the RDC purchased 42 acres of land at the end of Streetsbrook Road from the Rev. Henry Couchman in 1911 for £6,300. Robin Hood Cemetery opened on 26 September 1917. A chapel was built in 1931 and a crematorium was added to the chapel in 1958. In 1992 a new

97   Solihull Rural District Council, *c.*1930.

cemetery opened in Widney Manor Road because there was no space for new graves at Robin Hood.

The local population increased considerably following the creation of the RDC, but the sub-urban growth was not universally welcomed. An article in *Solihull Parish Magazine* of 1892 complained that 'speculative builders are beginning to look at Solihull and menace its open spaces. Hideous red brick houses are creeping gradually along the Warwick Road like a line of infantry invading the town.' The writer's opinion of the architecture of new houses appearing in the town was not shared by *White's Directory* of 1874, which had commented that many houses were 'large and handsome'.

The population of the parish was 3,739 in 1871 and had increased by only 462 since 1851. However, by 1901 it had increased to 7,517 and by 1921 was 11,552. This expansion was a factor in the reorganisation which created the Solihull

Urban District Council (UDC) in 1932. At this time the rural parishes of Lapworth, Bushwood and Tanworth were removed so that the UDC was a much smaller area than the RDC, although by 1931 the population of the proposed UDC had risen to 25,372.

The County Council retained responsibility for major services (although some were delegated to the UDC). Services administered by the UDC included: Allotments, Building Work, Cemeteries, Education (delegated), Food & Drugs, Highways, Housing, Health Services, Libraries (after 1947), Open Spaces, Town Planning and miscellaneous services such as Street Lighting, Sewage Disposal and Refuse Collection.

As an UDC Solihull was eligible to apply for its own coat of arms, but did not do so until 1946. A design was approved by the College of Arms and the Letters Patent were issued in September 1948. The design included two red stars from the coat of arms of the Oddingsells

98   Council House, Poplar Road, 1960s.

and a greyhound from those of the Greswolde family. It contained the Latin motto, 'Urbs in Rure' [the 'Town in the Country'].

The first Chairman of the UDC was Mr. Harry Charles Smith, who had served as Chairman of the RDC 1919-22. Charles Herbert Cook was appointed Clerk, William Gould Treasurer, Reginald Dunn Surveyor and Alfred Chard Sanitary Inspector. The scattered accommodation for staff was inadequate to meet the needs of the new local authority and there was still no dedicated place for the Council to meet. The UDC therefore decided to convert the Public Hall (which had eventually been acquired by the RDC) for use as the Council House.

The work involved constructing a Council Chamber and building an extension at the rear for office accommodation and was done by Epsley & Co, a building firm from Evesham, at a cost of £26,726. Some local firms were employed as sub-contractors. The work took some time and

99   General Election results, 1951: *left to right* Mrs. Joyce Lindsay, Martin Lindsay (MP), Maurice Mell, John Johnson (Labour Candidate), Mrs. Johnson.

some officers continued to work in houses near the Fire Station in Streetsbrook Road until the Council House opened in 1937.

100   Princess Margaret and Councillor R.D. Cooper, Charter Day, 1954.

Until 1945 Solihull was part of the Parliamentary Constituency of North Warwickshire but then a new constituency was created in time for the General Election. Martin Lindsay (1905-81), Conservative, was elected as the first MP for Solihull and remained as MP until 1964. A soldier, explorer and author, he inherited a baronetcy in 1962. The Labour Party candidate in 1945 was a young Royal Artillery captain called Roy Jenkins, who had been wounded at Dunkirk. Sir Winston Churchill visited Solihull on 25 June 1945 to canvass.

During the Second World War all non-essential building work ceased so that the tide of suburbanisation was temporarily halted. Construction materials remained scarce in the immediate post-war years but eventually materials became available again and the inexorable growth of the town continued. New roads such as Buryfield Road appeared in the former fields and the population continued to increase, reaching 72,470 by the early 1950s.

In 1954, recognising this continued expansion, Solihull was granted a charter creating Solihull Municipal Borough Council. This was a rise in status for the local authority, which retained the same boundaries as the UDC. Charter Day on 11 March 1954 was greeted with much celebration. Princess Margaret presented the Charter of Incorporation on behalf of her sister Queen Elizabeth II in a special ceremony held at the Odeon Cinema, Shirley. The Princess later appeared on the balcony of the Council House in Poplar Road to wave to the assembled crowds. Councillor R.D. Cooper, last Chairman of the UDC and Mayor designate, accepted the Charter.

Mr. W. Maurice Mell was appointed as the first Town Clerk. A programme of civic buildings was planned and the Civic Hall was the first to be completed. It was opened by Queen Elizabeth II on 25 May 1962. The Civic Hall was used for a

101 Last Council meeting in the old Council House, 1968.

wide range of activities such as dances (including the annual Mayor's Ball), performances by local drama groups, recitals and wrestling matches. More than a million people attended functions in the first two years alone. It was refurbished in 1983 and renamed Solihull Conference & Banqueting Centre, but was demolished in 1999 to make way for the Touchwood development.

A new Council House was the next project, opening in 1967. This building became known as Church Hill House when an extension was built in 1988 and named Orchard House. The Civic Suite was completed in 1968 and provided accommodation for the Council Chamber, Committee Rooms and the Mayor's Parlour. The original Council House in Poplar Road was leased to the Area Health Authority for many years. In 1999 it was converted for use as a wine bar and restaurant named Bar Censsa.

The population had continued to grow and more and more houses replaced former countryside. In 1964 Solihull was again promoted and became a County Borough (CB). The new Borough was responsible for administering all public services in the area. At this time the boundaries were changed and Hockley Heath was removed from Solihull CB.

The amazingly swift growth of Solihull and its fast progression as a local authority were noted by Sir Keith Joseph (then Minister for Housing and Local Government) in 1964 who wrote, 'Solihull is remarkable in its unparalleled rise in status and population over the last thirty years. It can claim to be unique in having such a success story'.

During all the rapid change in the 20th century Solihull had remained in Warwickshire but the most dramatic change came in the

102 Village water pump in Drury Lane, *c.*1870s.

1974 reorganisation of local government in England and Wales. Solihull was designated a Metropolitan Borough in the newly created County of the West Midlands, thus severing the link with Warwickshire which had lasted for centuries.

Solihull Metropolitan Borough Council (SMBC) covered a much larger geographical area than any of its predecessors and was formed by merging the old County Borough with part of Meriden Rural District Council. This added the rural area to the east of Solihull (including Balsall Common, Hampton-in-Arden, Berkswell, Barston and Meriden) and the urban areas of Marston Green, Chelmsley Wood, Kingshurst, Fordbridge

and Castle Bromwich. The village of Bickenhill with the adjacent National Exhibition Centre and Birmingham Airport were also contained in SMBC.

A new coat of arms in respect of the larger geographical area was granted in 1975. The design of the shield contains a black griffin from the arms of the Earl of Aylesford (a major landowner in Meriden), the greyhound from the Greswolde family of Malvern Hall and a fleur-de-lys from the arms of the Digby family who owned much of the Chelmsley Wood area. An oak tree at the top signifies the Forest of Arden, with sickles representing agriculture, and the original motto 'Urbs in rure' is repeated.

103   Solihull Gas Works, Wharf Lane, 1930s.

Another Parliamentary constituency was created in 1974 for the areas in the north and east of SMBC, with Solihull constituency continuing to represent the south-west areas. J.E. Tomlinson, representing Labour, was elected as the first MP and Iain Mills (Conservative) was elected in 1979, serving Meriden until his tragic death in 1997. Caroline Spelman (Conservative) is the MP at the time of writing (2001).

As early as 1874 *White's Directory* stated that the inhabitants of Solihull 'were well supplied with water and gas'. *Kelly's Directories* dated 1896 and 1900 record that water was supplied from wells but by 1908 state that water was supplied by Birmingham Water Works. Many residents continued to rely on a pump or a well to supply their water for many years, sometimes sharing the pump with neighbours. For example,

Ramsgate Cottages in Solihull High Street continued to use a communal pump until the late 1930s and this was replaced with one tap to serve all the cottages.

Solihull Gas Company was formed in 1869 and constructed a gasworks next to the *Grand Union Canal* about a mile north of Solihull town centre at a cost of £2,500. The coal required to make gas in the days before natural gas was piped from the North Sea was carried by barge along the canal. Eventually, coal was delivered by the railway and brought from Solihull Railway Station by carts and later by lorries. Gas was stored in large round gas holders, and was used mostly for lighting. Several photographs survive showing street lamps from different dates and recording changes in their design. The earliest lamps had to be lit each evening by a lamplighter who returned

104   Solihull Gas Works, *c.*1950.

each morning to switch them off. Most public houses had large decorative lamps over their main entrances to assist customers and attract trade. From 1877 the Gas Company had an office in the Lloyds Bank building in Poplar Road.

The Solihull RSA provided street lights and many residents introduced gas lighting into their homes (although most people installed gas lights only on the ground floor and continued to take candles upstairs). One or two very large houses such as Berry Hall built their own gas plant to provide a private supply. *Kelly's Directory* of 1928 is the first to mention electricity and states that

this was provided by the City of Birmingham Electric Supply Department.

By 1874 there was a 'fire engine station' belonging to the 'Birmingham Office' located in Drury Lane. A Solihull and District Volunteer Fire Brigade was formed in 1880, when a new fire engine was purchased by public subscription. The fire station was moved to a building in Warwick Road near the *Barley Mow*. Mr. Charles Bragg was the Captain in the 1880s and Mr. George Bragg was the Lieutenant. In 1896 the Brigade consisted of a captain and 13 men.

105 Solihull Fire Brigade with trophies from inter-district championship, *c*.1935.

In 1916 the fire engine was removed to Streetsbrook Road. A new Fire Station was opened in 1934, and this building has been considerably enlarged but was still in use in the year 2000.

Geoffrey Martineau recalled[2] many fires in the Solihull area in his lifetime. A dramatic fire occurred in 1866 at Silhill Hall Farm—all the barns and ricks were burnt but the house survived. Unfortunately the fire engine accidentally ran over its own hose as it turned into the farm gate—one fireman ran to the railway station to telegraph for assistance while messengers ran around the neighbours borrowing buckets and persuading people to join a line to pass buckets up and down. One helper was a gentleman in evening dress who had just returned from a dinner party. The farmer, however, restricted his endeavours to urging the helpers to work faster from his bedroom window before he returned to bed.

Problems were also encountered in January 1867 when Hillfield Hall caught fire. The weather was very cold and there was a heavy frost which caused the horses to slip on the icy roads, delaying their arrival, and the water in the fire engine froze. The original Elizabethan part of the house survived with some damage but the extensive additions made by the Feilding family were destroyed.

Fire struck the ricks again at Silhill Hall Farm in 1887 but no further damage was done on that occasion. The Hermitage in Lode Lane was badly damaged by fire during one night in 1905, but fortunately the entire household managed to escape just before the first floor collapsed. These fires were accidental but Geoffrey Martineau also recalled a case of arson when in 1912 suffragettes set fire to a house at the corner of Grange Road and Warwick Road.

106 Fire at the Hermitage, Lode Lane, 1905.

Bentley Manor was badly damaged by fire on 21 July 1911 and a fire damaged Widney Manor House in 1925 (the top storey was destroyed and never rebuilt) and 'Cow Hayes' near Ravenshaw was completely destroyed in the 1930s. This was a notorious event when the owner accused the firemen who attended the fire of getting drunk on some of the contents of the wine cellar and allowing the house to burn. Some firemen were dismissed as a result.

The first Police Station in Solihull was built in New Road in 1851 and served both as a house for the police officer and his family and as a lock-up. At that time there were no other buildings in New Road. The building was extended in 1857 and provided accommodation on the ground floor for two cells and an office on one side of the building and a kitchen and parlour on the other side. In addition there was a yard with a scullery, pantry and lavatory for the family and an enclosed Prisoners' Yard for exercise. The first floor contained two further cells and three bedrooms.

By 1874 the local police force consisted of Inspector Jesse Welch and eight police constables. The original lock-up served until 1892 when a new police station was built in Poplar Road. The old building was converted for use as a house

and later the ground floor became shop accommodation. Various businesses have been located there including a post office, a hairdresser's, an antique shop and a shop selling air-conditioning systems.

The Police Station in Poplar Road was much larger and provided accommodation for the growing number of policemen required for the expanding town. By 1896 William Carbis was recorded as Superintendent of the Solihull Division with one inspector, five sergeants and 31 constables under his command. Poplar Road Police Station was in use from 1892 until 1970 when a new Police Station opened in Homer Road.

A long and distinguished line of doctors has served the town's residents. A house survives in Warwick Road opposite Poplar Road where a succession of doctors lived from 1761-1974 including Thomas Lowe, Adolphus Bernays, St John Whitehouse, and Paul and Doris Quinet. The house was called 'The Limes' but was often referred to as the 'Doctor's House' and was renamed in honour of the Quinets, its last residents. The building is now used as office accommodation.

The Page family contributed to medical service in the town for more than a century. Dr.

107 Superintendent Carbis (*centre*) and Solihull Police, 1920.

Edward Sutton Page (see illustration 51) came to Solihull in 1866 to be the assistant to the surgeon Thomas Lowe and took over the medical practice when Mr. Lowe retired. Edward (who died in 1912) held most of the important medical positions in Solihull during his long career, including appointments to Solihull Union Workhouse, Solihull Infectious Hospital, Evans Convalescent Home, Solihull and Tanworth Districts, the police and the Great Western Railway. It was his proud boast that he had 'attended 9,000 patients in childbirth and never had the misfortune to lose a mother'.

Edward Page had a large family, which included a son called Shirley who qualified as a doctor but died in 1904 aged only 30, less than a year after his elder brother Gilbert had died. Another son, Ferdinand, also followed in his father's footsteps and for many years until 1936 practised medicine from his home at the Manor House in the High Street. Ferdinand was followed in turn by his son Erichsen who had a practice in Herbert Road, Solihull until the 1960s.

Dr. Adolphus Bernays was in practice in the village for many years. He held his practice (which still exists in 2001 as Bernays & Whitehouse with a surgery in Union Road, Shirley) at the 'Doctor's House' and also at a house called the 'Gables' in

108 Harvey Chattock (1819-98), landowner and magistrate.

109   Doctor's House, Warwick Road with Coronation arch, 1911.

110   Dr. Ferdinand Page.

the High Street. A wealthy man, Bernays was one of the first motorists in the village and owned a succession of vehicles, employing Joseph Fripp as a chauffeur (see illustration 56).

Belgian-born Paul Quinet first visited Solihull when he stayed with Dr. Whitehouse during vacations from the boarding school where he had been sent by his father for safety during the First World War. With the exception of serving in the Belgian army in 1918-9 Paul was to spend the remainder of his life in Solihull. He married Doris Wilcox from Fowgay Hall in Dingle Lane, having met her when they were both studying medicine at Birmingham University.

Paul and Doris often worked together especially when performing operations (when Doris acted as anaesthetist). In the 1920-30s minor operations were often carried out at the patient's home, and Doris later recalled occasions when a fire had been lit in the room to be used—this was unfortunate at a time when inflammable chloroform was commonly used as an anaesthetic. Paul held many medical appointments in Solihull during the Second World War (more details appear in Chapter 9) and worked at Solihull

111 Welfare Food Campaign, 1953.

Hospital until his official retirement in 1965, although he continued to work as a locum until 1972. He died in 1978, having suffered ill health for a number of years. Doris served as a councillor for some years in the 1930s and was the only female councillor at the time Solihull was awarded Borough status in 1954. She continued to live at their last home in Lode Lane for many years and died in a nursing home in 1990.

Nurses and midwives served the local community alongside the doctors. Most children were born at home until the mid-20th century. Mrs. Webb from Deebank's Yard in Warwick Road was one of many midwives in the village, serving for many years.

The village chemists played an important role in delivering medical services; many villagers could not afford to pay for a doctor so would ask the chemist to suggest a remedy. Chemists in the High Street have included Edwin Trinder, who had a shop at the corner of the High Street and Mill Lane, and Mr. Winfield, who had a shop near the Square and later moved to the corner of Poplar Road (where the shop was damaged in an air raid in the Second World War).

Traditional remedies were still practised in the 19th century and Geoffrey Martineau remembered a Miss Lane, who lived with her brother William (a water carrier) in Mill Lane and kept a supply of leeches to take to the sick.

Solihull Union Workhouse already provided an infirmary ward by 1866 when Edward Page arrived in the village, although the ward had only six beds each for men and women at that time. The workhouse was gradually extended and more provision was made for the sick until the site eventually stretched from Union Road to Lode Lane.

The Solihull Board of Guardians was abolished in 1926 and control passed first to Warwick County Council and then in 1948 to the National Health Service. The Infirmary was designated an emergency hospital during the Second World War under the supervision of Paul Quinet and dealt with war casualties, orthopaedics, midwifery and gynaecology and became Solihull Hospital after the War.

In 1863 a convalescent home for sick children was established and maintained in Warwick Road at her own expense by Caroline Martineau. The children originally came from West Bromwich

112   Solihull Clinic, Drury Lane, 1960.

but patients from Birmingham Children's Hospital were soon accepted. Miss Martineau gave the house to the institution in 1872 and left Solihull. The administration of the home was then undertaken

113   Evans Convalescent Home, Widney Manor Road.

by Mrs. Evans, wife of Canon Charles Evans, Rector of Solihull 1872-94. Mrs. Evans raised money for the Home by inviting charitable subscriptions and by 1880 approximately 90 people were giving annual subscriptions of five to ten shillings, although Joseph Gillott of Berry Hall gave two guineas and his wife gave five pounds. A new building was erected in Widney Manor Road by 1887 which continued until 5 July 1948 when the Home passed to state control under the terms of the National Health Act 1946.

A private clinic was established in a house called Northmeade in Station Road. A clinic was set up by the NHS in a temporary building in Drury Lane in 1945. In the early 1960s the clinic moved to a house on the site now occupied by Solihull Library and opened in a purpose-built clinic in Grove Road in 1971. A private hospital, Solihull Parkway, opened in 1982 in Damson Parkway and is now operated by BUPA.

Seven

Housing

The dwellings in the manor of Ulverlei would have been made of wattle and daub with thatched roofs. By the middle ages timber was used extensively in Warwickshire as a building material. Buildings were made from a framework of timber with the spaces filled in with wattle and daub. By the Elizabethan period brick was also used as an infill material.

Moats became a feature for larger, isolated houses in the middle ages. The moats may have had several purposes including defence, fish farming and status symbols.

Silhill Hall, formerly situated at the corner of Streetsbrook Road and Broad Oaks Road, dated from the 14th century and originally consisted of a great hall with cross wings and a moat. Alterations were made at various dates from the 16th century but the house survived until 1966 when, although a Grade I listed building, it was illegally demolished by its owner.

Ravenshaw Hall was built in the early 15th century near a ford on the River Blythe. Its name means 'the wood of the ravens' and was first recorded in 1591 in a land revenue list. Originally

114 Typical timber-framed cottages: Nos. 7-9 Hampton Lane, *c.*1956.

115   Silhill Hall, Streetsbrook Road.

116   Conjectural drawing of Silhill Hall by J.A. Cossins, *c.*1890.

moated, the house consisted of a great hall with wings for the solar and buttery. Old Berry Hall in Ravenshaw Lane was built in the late 15th century and from 1505 to 1671 was the home of the Waring family. Although some of the original timber-framed building has been long demolished the house has retained its moat. Ravenshaw and Berry Hall are now listed Grade II and Grade II*.

Dovehouse Farm (see illustration 18) in Dovehouse Lane dates from around 1500 and was built in an L-shape. Part of the front of the timber-framed house was later faced with brick. The Lea family farmed at Dovehouse in the early 20th century and the house was lovingly restored by the Luntley family in the 1960s. Although omitted from the original *List of Buildings of Special Historic or Architectural Interest*, it was eventually listed Grade II* in 1972.

Witley Farm, later known as Malvern Park Farm (see illustration 8), is a timber-framed house built in Widney Manor Road in the late 16th century. Originally built in an L-shape, the timber-framed house was later extended in brick to fill in the space in the L and is now listed

117 Libbards House, *c.*1970.

Grade II*. Members of the Lea family also farmed at Malvern Park.

Some of these timber-framed farmhouses were replaced in the 18th century by large, elegant brick houses such as 'Southend' in Homer Road and Libbards House near Widney Manor Road. Fortunately Libbards survives, having been converted into flats in the 1980s.

At least three buildings have housed the rectors of Solihull. The earliest known was a timber-framed building with several gables. The last of a succession of incumbents to live in this house was the notorious Charles Curtis (Rector 1789-1829). Irving van Wart knew Parson Curtis in his old age and described[1] him as follows:

> The old rector ... presented a goodly picture as he rode down the carriage-road. His smooth Saxon countenance showed no furrows of age, though creases of jolly fat round his rubicund cheeks evinced that good living was his example as well as precept. His portly and sleek proportions well became his clerical shovel hat, white cravat, and ample black coat

118 Solihull Rectory, pre-1933.

119   High Street with the Manor House (*right*), pre-1931.

and vest; while drab kersey breeches and old-fashioned top-boots completed his costume in his double character as a sporting parson.

The lovely old rectory was demolished by Curtis's successor Archer Clive (Rector 1829-47) after he had built a large new house in 1833 at his own expense. Archer's house was built with bricks specially made in a field near the site, which saved him 11 shillings for every thousand bricks.

Archer was the grandson of the last Lord Archer of Umberslade Hall and, although a second son, was a relatively wealthy man. During his time at Solihull Archer became friends with the heiress and writer Caroline Meysey Wigley, who first came to Solihull in 1829 when her brother Edmund inherited Malvern Hall from their cousin Henry Greswolde Lewis. Edmund changed his name to Greswolde as a condition of the bequest, but did not long enjoy his inheritance, dying of cholera in 1833 when in Ireland with his regiment.

Caroline inherited Olton Hall, a large 18th-century mansion in Lode Lane, now the site of the *Olton Tavern*, where she lived until 1840 when she married Archer Clive and moved to his new house, renting Olton Hall to her cousin 'Gumley Wilson' for £260 a year for 20 years. Caroline was disabled from a childhood illness but did not allow this to deter her from leading an active life, which included visiting family and friends and travelling abroad. Wilson left a vivid description of her in his autobiography:[2]

> Miss Wigley was a cripple - that is, was in irons as to her legs, but rode about all over the country unattended and used to get awful falls now and then, but her pluck was indomitable. We were the greatest of friends ...She was very well read, very clever and a very charming companion, but was not in her first youth ... Archer Clive, a fine handsome young man, under forty, got the living [of Solihull Church]. He also was very

120   High Street with 'handsome' houses, *c*.1910.

well read and very clever. She succumbed and married her pastor and a very happy marriage it turned out. There was a similarity of taste and opinions which certainly conduces to happiness in that state.

Archer and Caroline lived very happily in Solihull Rectory with their son and daughter until the death of Archer's father, shortly after the sudden death of his elder brother. This event meant that Archer inherited the Clive family estate and the family moved to Herefordshire, leaving Solihull Rectory to his successors who continued to live there for many years.

The Victorian house was very large and most rectors employed several servants. The Rev. T.B. Harvey Brooks was the rector 1894-1926 and often let the house in the summer. Mr. Harvey Brooks was succeeded as rector by his son-in-law Charles Wormald, who had been appointed Deacon at St Alphege Church in 1903 and was ordained while serving as a curate in Solihull.

Charles left Solihull in 1909 and changed his name to Wormald from Wormell, possibly because of jokes about his original name, before he married Ada Wynifred Harvey Brooks in August 1910. By the time Charles and Wynifred returned to live in her old home they had four children.

The Victorian rectory was becoming increasingly expensive to maintain and servants were difficult to recruit after the First World War when more opportunities were available to women. In June 1932 Mr. Wormald wrote in the *Parish Magazine* that the house 'was an impossible family home' and therefore decided to build a smaller house in 1933 adjacent to the old rectory which was then demolished, having served for a hundred years as the home of five successive rectors.

The house now known as the Manor House in Solihull High Street was built in the late 15th century by the Greswold family. The close-set timber frame has four gables and the top storey originally protruded beyond the line of the ground floor. This jettied top storey was later filled in with brickwork and casement windows. Never actually the home of the lords of the manor, the house was known by the 19th century as Lime Tree House from the nine trees planted outside the house around 1720. Three of the trees survived until the mid-20th century.

Thomas Horne lived at the Manor House for many years until about 1910. The 1891 census described him as a 69-year-old retired brass founder born in Aston, Warwickshire, living alone with two servants (Emma Lifley and Fanny Evans). Several former residents have recorded memories of Mr. Horne, who used to like to stand or sit at the door of the Manor House watching the world go by while smoking his churchwarden pipe.

Dr. Ferdinand Page followed Thomas Horne and was to be the last resident of the house, which was bought by a brewery in 1938. Plans to convert the building into a public house were changed by the outbreak of the Second World War and the house was finally offered for sale in 1944. A trust was formed which raised £12,000 by 1945 to buy the house and still administers it, which is now a Grade II listed building.

The timber-framed building recently used (until 1999) as the *Raison d'Etre* wine bar was probably built in 1571 and is also listed Grade II. It was known as Harborne House in the 19th century, when a brick-built 'gothic' style porch had been added. Hawkesford's corn chandler's and seed merchant's shop occupied part of the building from 1896 to 1912.

Gradually brick replaced timber as a building material and elegant houses were built in the town, often replacing earlier timber-framed buildings. By the late 19th century many of these houses had gained porches and some were covered in ivy or wisteria.

The original house known as the Priory (see illustration 91) stood at the top of Church Hill, opposite the west end of St Alphege Church, and was a large timber-framed building probably dating from at least the 16th century. Its name was allegedly acquired after its owner sheltered the nuns from Henwood when their nunnery was dissolved at the Reformation. It was still the home of a prominent local Roman Catholic, Hugford Hassall, in the 18th century. Mr. Hassall

was a friend of Joseph Weston, who was the organist at St Alphege Church and would sometimes slip out during the sermon on Sundays to drink a glass of wine with his friend—unfortunately he did not always arrive back before the end of the sermon.

The Priory housed John Powell's private school from 1780 to 1840 which was the school attended by Irving van Wart, who later described[3] his first impressions of the house:

> Opposite the parsonage house is an irregular rough-cast house, with red tiled gable roof … This was formerly a large farm-house, but for years past had been occupied by a school. …We entered a wide, square hall, with quarry floor and ample hearth, which had been the common sitting-room in the days of the farm; and by a passage thence to a wainscoted parlour, a snug, old-fashioned apartment overlooking the playground. … He conducted me over the house; pointing out the study commanding the church, which we should all share in common; thence by a passage from the main hall, to the entrance of an ample kitchen, where buxom maids were ever busy.

In the 1880s the Priory was bought by the Matthews family who had been living at St Bernard's Grange, Olton. Mr. Matthews decided to build a new house and demolish the old one. The new Priory was built of brick, with decorative wood work, and was ready by 1889. The Matthews were the only family to live in the new Priory—it was used for various services (including Solihull Library from the 1950s to 1976 when the new Central Library opened) and now houses voluntary organisations such as the Citizens' Advice Bureau and Solihull Talking Newspaper.

Touchwood Hall was a red-brick building in Drury Lane dating from around 1712 but probably replacing an earlier moated house. The remains of the moat were adjacent to common land and were used as a horse pool for many years. Touchwood was the home of the Holbeche, Madeley and Martineau families in turn. The origins of the name are unknown. The Hall was demolished in the early 1960s when Mell Square was built but its name lives on in Touchwood Hall Close off Lode Lane and in the shopping development due to open in September 2001.

The Madeleys owned a tannery in Warwick Road in the mid-19th century until it was closed

121   Touchwood Hall, Drury Lane, *c.*1910.

by Charles Madeley in 1867. His mother and unmarried sisters continued to live at Touchwood and Charles built himself a new house. His sisters Ellen and Caroline Madeley were still living in the house in 1891 when they were aged 75 and 59 respectively.

Eventually Charles's fourth daughter Jessie moved into Touchwood Hall after her marriage to Geoffrey Martineau (whose reminiscences are quoted throughout this book). Jessie and Geoffrey were married in St Alphege Church on Saturday, 4 January 1896 and the event was reported in the *Solihull & District Monthly Magazine.* The bride 'was attired in a rich white silk dress with tulle veil' and her youngest sister Nellie was the brides-maid wearing a white silk dress trimmed with tulle and a large black hat (possibly a reference to the fact that their father had died three months earlier). The bride was given away by her brother, Charles Junior, and the bridegroom's brother,

Alfred, was the best man. The magazine recorded that:

> A large number of people assembled in the church to witness the ceremony, for both bride and groom are members of two of the oldest Solihull families and are very popular, having for a number of years taken an active part in the Sunday Schools, where they have gained the love and confidence of the children. ... The happy pair left Solihull early in the day *en route* for Bournemouth where the honeymoon will be spent.

Geoffrey Martineau had founded the Solihull Guild of Amateur Bellringers in 1891 and had helped to restore the practice of bellringing in Solihull Parish Church. Geoffrey and Jessie had a son, Clement, who died in France during the First World War. Geoffrey died in 1934, leaving his memoirs in the parish magazine unfinished, but Jessie survived until 1947.

122   Cottages in Park Road, pre-1931.

123   Cottages in Warwick Road, pre-1935, later the site of the Magistrates' Court.

124   Cottage in Warwick Road with Mrs. Elizabeth Turner.

Many timber-framed cottages survived into the 20th century, including several in Mill Lane, Drury Lane and Park Road. Brick cottages survived in several places including Warwick Road near Drury Lane at Tainters Green and at the junction of Lode Lane and Poplar Road. This area was known as Golden End in the early 19th century and may have been the location of a market. The cottages were demolished in 1935 to make way for the first Magistrates' Court building (magistrates had used various locations including the *George Hotel* and the Old Town Hall).

Poplar House was a picturesque house opposite Poplar Road and took its name from the 21 Lombardy poplar trees in the garden. For many years the home of Doris Hamilton Smith and her family, the house was demolished to make way for Brueton Gardens, which were the gift of Horace Brueton as a memorial after the First World War, and the family moved to 'Hazlewood' in Homer Road.

After Solihull Railway Station opened in 1852 many new houses were built to accommodate the families who were attracted to the town. In the late 19th and early 20th centuries handsome villas were built in Warwick Road and in country lanes such as Lode Lane, School Lane, Homer Road and Herbert Road. These large houses attracted

125   Poplar House, at the corner of Warwick Road and Lode Lane, *c.*1900.

126   19th-century villas in Warwick Road, *c.*1916.

127   Mr. and Mrs. Cull and family in Lugtrout Lane, *c.*1910.

128   'Church View', School Lane, *c.*1910.

middle-class residents who were often able to employ servants.

Some larger houses were also built, such as Tudor Grange in Blossomfield Road, which was built for Birmingham businessman Alfred Lovekin and later sold to Alfred Bird of Bird's Custard fame.

Building work was halted during the First World War but considerable development took place in the 1920-30s when a variety of houses were built, including semi-detached properties. New estates were created at this time, such as the Rectory Road estate built on land near the bottom of Church Hill formerly belonging to Solihull Rectory.

The local authority also began to build houses, many of which were located in Alston Road, Cornyx Lane and Hermitage Road. Development came to a halt once again at the outbreak of the Second World War and was slow to resume in the late 1940s because building materials were

129 Typical parlour maid, *c.*1910.

130 'Hazlewood', Homer Road, 1913.

131   No.3 Lode Lane, pre-1964.

132   No.739 Warwick Road, *c*.1956.

133   No.86 Alston Road, interior.

difficult to obtain. To overcome the housing shortage temporary 'pre-fabs' were constructed by the local authority in the Hobs Moat area, with the first dwellings officially opened by Martin Lindsay MP on 10 November 1945. Permanent houses later replaced the 'pre-fabs'.

Considerable development took place in the last 50 years of the 20th century so that the character of the area is now entirely suburban, although several parks, open spaces and fragments of woodland survive as reminders of a more rural past.

134   No.86 Alston Road.

135   Temporary 'prefab'—No.8 Jasmine Lane, 1950s.

Eight

Social Life and Entertainment

The concept of leisure time is relatively modern for all except the very wealthy. In the middle ages Sundays and holy days afforded some free time for ordinary people. Fairs were often associated with holy days and Solihull had an annual three-day fair coinciding with the feast day of St Alphege in April. In addition to merchants and pedlars selling their wares, entertainment was also on offer—itinerant musicians, acrobats and jugglers competed for attention with dancing bears and there was always the opportunity to hear news spread by travellers. The weekly market also offered a forum for exchanging news and gossip with friends and neighbours.

The fairs continued into the 19th century and were held in the Square, where roundabouts were in place and swing boats flew up into the lime trees surrounding the churchyard. A photograph survives showing two sad, muzzled, performing bears with their trainer at a fair in the Square. Charles Lines remembered[1] his mother's memories of the fair and in particular a long-standing disagreement with her sister about which of them had insisted on taking a ride on a roundabout (with unfortunate consequences).

Gradually, seasonal activities became customary, such as Christmas festivities and May Day revels when chimney sweeps toured the area with the 'Jack-in-the-Green' (a large wicker frame covered in green boughs in which a boy was concealed) and dances took place around the Maypole.

136 May Day, 1878.

137 A circus in the Square, *c*.1910.

These activities, and the annual fairs, were disapproved of by Canon Evans, Rector of Solihull 1872-94, because they attracted large numbers of people. Many of these visitors came from Birmingham (often referred to as 'Brumagem') and some were considered 'undesirable', so the Rector caused the fair to be discontinued.

Circuses later made regular visits to the town, often setting up in Malvern Park or on fields near the bottom of Church Hill. Charles Lines remembered[2] being taken by his grandfather to Sanger's Circus in Malvern Park and advertisements appeared in *Warwick County News* in the 1930-40s for Sir Robert Fossett's Circus (with 'ponderous elephants, the Flying Demons, the Cossack Riders and Isabel, Queen of the Circus') and for Paulo's Royal Circus ('A Show of Thrills and Talent').

Groups of itinerant players appeared from time to time and local tradition states that ancient Dog Lane changed its name to Drury Lane after a performance was held in a barn at Touchwood Hall.

By the early 19th century the gentry and the emerging middle classes had spare time for recreation. Irving van Wart described[3] local society at that times as follows:

> The rector and his curate, a few ancient spinsters and retired officers, who lived in economical gentility—the doctor, lawyer and country-squire, formed the aristocracy of the neighbourhood, composed principally of small farmers.

Assemblies were held at the Old Town Hall in the Square and private dances were held at the larger houses. Dinner parties were held where guests would also have the opportunity to exchange news and play whist and other card games.

138   The Matthews family at the seaside, *c*.1890.

The Rev. Archer Clive began to keep a diary[4] in 1838 in which he recorded social engagements in addition to parish duties and private thoughts. He often recorded visits to his family in Herefordshire or London and dining in Solihull with friends, including local clergy such as the Rev. Patrick Smythe at Tanworth-in-Arden and Miss Caroline Meysey Wigley who lived at Olton Hall.

In March 1838 Archer went to Birmingham with Caroline, Dr. Cowrie and Lady Wallace to see a play but was not impressed: 'Our places had been reserved a week before but the sovereign people took possession and we were glad to find places in a back row. Then the Gallery, what with fighting and hollowing, did not suffer a word of the performance to be heard. As for the police, there was no attempt at it.' Although Archer was not inclined to visit a theatre in

Birmingham again he went to the opera when in London.

Archer and Caroline were married in 1840 and Archer's diary became a joint effort, although Caroline contributed the greater share. The Clives continued to entertain relatives, friends and neighbours to dinner, often followed by music or card games, and gave occasional balls for tenants, servants and tradesfolk. They also took holidays in England, Scotland and on the Continent.

The Rev. Harvey Brooks often included a letter in the *Parish Magazine* to inform his parishioners of his holiday arrangements. He usually holidayed in England or Scotland but occasionally travelled abroad, sometimes for his health.

Rare family photographs from the 1880s survive in an album from the Matthews family, who lived at St Bernard's Grange in Olton and later at the Priory, showing the family at the seaside. One photograph shows bathing machines while others include the children riding donkeys on the beach or rowing in a small boat.

Most families did not have the means to take a holiday but by the late 19th century Sundays and bank holidays provided new opportunities for leisure activities. Day excursions were also popular. In July 1894 James Leal, a draper in the High Street, advertised his 'Annual Excursion' in the *Parish Magazine*. The destination was to be Bournemouth, Southampton and Portsmouth on 15 August and 'early application for tickets' was advised.

Many local organisations, often from various churches, also arranged outings. On Friday, 29 July 1898 the choir adults and the bell ringers from St Alphege Church journeyed to Church Stretton—by train from Solihull to Shrewsbury (taking just two and a quarter hours) and by horse-drawn 'brake' for the last 14 miles. On the previous Saturday the choir boys were taken by the organist Mr. Courtenay Woods on an outing to Oxford, where they visited colleges, had dinner and tea, went swimming and rowed on the river.

Parks also offered opportunities for leisure and recreation. Malvern Park was formerly part of the private deer park belonging to Malvern Hall and was purchased by the local authority in the 1920s. Horace Brueton bought the remaining land, but sold Malvern Hall for use as the High School and built houses in Brueton Avenue and

139 The Hawkins family in Brueton Park, *c*.1953.

Park Avenue. In 1944 Mr. Brueton gave his land for use as a public park.

Solihull has long enjoyed organisations devoted to cultural activities. Archer and Caroline Clive both mention[5] a Book Club. As early as 6 June 1838 Archer wrote ironically to Caroline, who was touring in France with her maid for company (this was before the couple were engaged to be married), 'Whatever you may be doing next Monday pray remember that you are losing the delights of the Solihull Book Club'. That meeting was not a great success for Archer who recorded in his diary, 'Book-club ... society small and select—bloody genteel—"the curate's wife with all her graces"'.

After they married Archer and Caroline often read books together and were remarkably broad-minded, including Rabelais among their selections. Caroline had literary ambitions and published several volumes of poetry and novels. The Clives met Robert and Elizabeth Browning on their travels in Italy.

A Reading Room and Library was established in Solihull High Street in 1883, funded by subscriptions and a generous donation from the Rector, Canon Evans. The *Parish Magazine* for December 1883 reported that,

> Commodious premises having at length been secured, in High Street, an excellent reading room, well supplied with daily papers, has been opened ... [plus] a circulating library, from which a constant supply of new books, supplied by Messrs Mudie, can be obtained for the modest subscription of 10s. and 6d. per annum.

The accounts, published in December 1884, showed that the costs for the first year were £71 10s. 11d.

140   Solihull Reading Room & Library and Mrs. Lines' shop, High Street, *c.*1896.

December 1883 also saw the launch of Solihull Literary Society with Canon Evans announced as President. The committee included leading Silhillians such as Harvey Chattock, Dr. Bernays and Canon O'Sullivan (the Roman Catholic priest). The programme listed lectures by 'eminent men', members' nights and a 'Conversazione'. The inaugural meeting was a lecture on 'The Antiquities of Solihull' by the President.

Musical activities have played an important part in the social life of the village for many years. Caroline Clive often mentioned musical events in her diaries. These were often impromptu performances after dinner, but she also belonged to a musical society and recorded several squabbles between members.

In the late 19th century Charles Hopkins, who had a barber's shop at the corner of Drury Lane and High Street, used to earn a supplementary income by playing music for private dances on his violin accompanied by his daughter on the harp. James Holliday, the last Parish beadle, and his wife used to act as Master of Ceremonies and Cloakroom attendant for parties. Concerts were given by various organisations and individuals, including Squire Alston of Elmdon Hall, who sometimes allowed concerts to be held in outbuildings belonging to Elmdon Hall. A brass band had been formed by 1887 which participated in many local events. A Musical Festival was held in 1871.

The dramatic arts were also catered for, with entertainments staged at venues such as the Public Hall in Poplar Road and Church House, built in Drury Lane in 1885. The *Parish Magazine* contains details of many societies active in the late 19th

141 Fancy dress dance at the Public Hall, Poplar Road, with William Johnson (*in dinner jacket centre*), 1920s.

and early 20th centuries. Solihull Science & Art Association had been created by 1894 and was publishing an interesting programme of lectures.

By 1944 many activities seem to have ceased and a small group of people decided to create a society to foster the arts in Solihull. The original idea grew out of a casual conversation one Sunday between Lady Robert Bird (daughter-in-law of Sir Alfred Bird) and Dr. Richard Wassell, organist at St Alphege Church. Dr. Wassell was a distinguished musician and wished to introduce 'first class' concerts, a choral society and a competitive musical festival. Lady Bird and others wished to cater for drama and art.

Solihull Society of Arts published its first programme for September 1944 when it had set up Drama, Music and Literary and Debating Sections. It was always the intention that the

Society should grow and further sections were added including: the Art Section in 1959, Connoisseurs' Circle (later Antiques Circle) 1972, Recorded Music Circle 1981 and the Local History Circle (founded in 1987 by the late Charles Lines and the author).

Other societies catered for horticulture, chrysanthemums and amateur gardening and there were annual flower and produce shows. Several churches had needlework and embroidery groups.

Social gatherings often had charitable motives. Fund-raising events such as fêtes and bazaars would be organised from time to time for various projects, often under the auspices of one of the churches. For example, Mrs. Evans (wife of the Rector) organised a 'Grand Village Fayre' in the Rectory gardens in 1883 to raise money for the Evans Children's Convalescent

142 Solihull Flower Show, *c*.1905.

143 Garden Party in Ashleigh Road. *Front row left to right* Dr. Bernays, Gertrude Lawrence and Douglas Fairbanks Jnr., *c*.1935.

Home which attracted more than 2,000 visitors and raised over £350. Stalls offering china, fine arts, toys and fancy goods were erected in a marquee and the entertainment included Punch and Judy, a maypole, a tennis tournament and

'Aunt Sally'. The event opened with a grand procession of 'lady stall holders' accompanied by village children in historical costumes and led by the Fire Brigade and the village brass band.

Garden parties were popular events, often with a charitable object. A garden party was held in aid of the RSPCA at a house in Ashleigh Road *c*.1935, which was attended by local residents and visiting celebrities. The Rectory garden was often the venue for events such as a garden party held by local Freemasons on 18 September 1937 in aid of the church restoration fund. Unfortunately the weather was 'wet and somewhat cold', so that many people bought tickets but did not attend.

There have been branches of national organisations in Solihull such as the Oddfellows (founded *c*.1840) and the Caledonian Corks. One of three branches of the Becher Club, a friendly society founded by the Rev. J. Becher of Stockwell in Northamptonshire, was started in 1848. The other branches were located in Alcester

144   The Oddfellows at
the *George Hotel*.

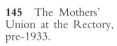

145   The Mothers'
Union at the Rectory,
pre–1933.

146   Solihull Carnival,
1935.

147   The *Golden Lion*, Warwick Road, *c*.1897.

and Straford-upon-Avon. The Oddfellows, Caledonian Corks and the Becher Club had large, ceremonial banners which were proudly carried in processions around the town in honour of national events and their own anniversaries.

The first carnival in Solihull took place in 1932. Mary Grace Bragg was voted Carnival Queen and had a King and attendants, all clothed in splendid robes. A procession of decorated floats paraded around the town. The Rector, Charles Wormald, recorded in the *Parish Magazine* that

'the whole thing was an example of perfect organization, performed in a very happy way. Never before, I am sure, have such crowds been seen in Solihull.'

Public houses have often been the venue for social gatherings, both formal an informal. For example, Henry Edginton, landlord of the *Golden Lion* in Warwick Road, staged an ox-roast to celebrate the Diamond Jubilee of Queen Victoria in 1897. Some of the older establishments had been coaching inns until the advent of the railway

148 The *Gardener's Arms*, High Street, 1904.

removed the trade. The *Barley Mow, George, Royal Oak* and *Golden Lion* were former coaching inns but managed to remain in business as public houses.

The *George* was regarded more as a meeting place for the gentry. Miss Doris Hamilton Smith, a lifelong resident of Solihull, recalled that she would sometimes be taken to the hotel for luncheon 'but one would never visit a public house'. The *George* probably dates from the 16th century and has been known as the *Nag's Head* (1693-1715) and the *Bell* (1715-38). A Grade II listed building, it was heavily restored *c.*1991 and is now (2001) owned by Jarvis Hotels.

The brick-built *Masons Arms* in the High Street dates from the early 19th century and the *Malt Shovel* (now *Rosie O'Briens*) was originally timber-framed, although now only the façade remains. The *Royal Oak Hotel* was situated at the corner of High Street and Drury Lane until its

demolition in the early 1960s. The *Gardener's Arms* was located in the High Street from the 1860s to 1971, when it too was demolished. An infamous murder took place in the backyard in 1880 when John Gateley was shot dead by a fellow Irishman. Recent research has shown that the murderer was apprehended in London some years later and brought to trial. He was found guilty of manslaughter, not murder, but given a lengthy sentence.

Blood sports are now regarded with distaste by many people, but hunting was a recreational activity for wealthier residents in the past. In the Middle Ages the Forest of Arden was not a forest in strict legal terms, where game was the property of the Crown under forest law, so the local lords of manors and their families and friends probably hunted using hounds and falcons.

Foxhunting has a long history in Warwickshire. The North Warwickshire Hunt

149   Solihull Bowling Green, *George Hotel*, *c*.1900.

was created in 1791 under its first Master John Corbett (who had hunted at Meriden since 1788). The Rev. Charles Curtis, Rector of Solihull 1789-1829, was a notable local huntsman. He was also Rector of Birmingham 1781-1829, but preferred to live at Solihull. As there was no organised local hunt he often joined neighbours to hunt fox and hare. From about 1811 he employed Joe Pitchford as his huntsman and kept a pack of harriers in Drury Lane.

In his youth Curtis had a reputation as a reckless rider but in his old age could not always keep up with the hunt. On one famous occasion he is alleged to have shouted to Joe Pitchford as the other riders left him behind, 'If you catch him I'll eat him!' and a cartoon later appeared in Vyner's *Notitia Venatica* (a national publication) showing the fox being served at 'Parson Curtis' Dinner Party'—it was not recorded whether the unfortunate animal was actually eaten.

William 'Gumley' Wilson was another well-known local huntsman. His family owned Knowle Hall and estates in Leicestershire but he squandered so much of his own and his family's fortunes that he sold Knowle Hall and rented Olton Hall in Lode Lane, which belonged to his cousin, Caroline Clive. 'Gumley' with the help of his servants eventually emigrated to America to escape the debtors' prison. In his autobiography[6] he attributed his downfall to his lack of self discipline, never going without any luxury that he craved, and also to his inability to deny a pretty woman anything she wanted. Much of his fortune was spent on horses for hunting and racing and on chorus girls.

Horse races were held at several locations in the Solihull area from the late 18th century. An anonymous newspaper cutting announces 'Solihull Races' on Monday, 18 September 1780 when a purse of 50 guineas was offered as a prize. Races were held from around 1830-40, for example as announced in the *Warwick & Warwickshire Advertiser* of 19 September 1835 near the *Seven Star Inn* in Warwick Road. This was probably held on land owned by Thomas Chattock and rented to Hugh Taylor of the *George Hotel* for this purpose.

By 1879 races were advertised at 'a race-course a mile from Olton Station'—possibly on farmland which later became Olton Golf Course in Dovehouse Lane. Another racecourse opened on Stratford Road, Shirley, around 1900 and finally closed in 1953.

The game of bowls is probably one of the oldest sporting activities in Britain and a form of the game was popular by the 13th century. The oldest bowling club in England is believed to be Southampton, which claims to have been founded in 1299. Bowls were actually forbidden for many years because playing the game interfered with archery practice. Private greens were permitted by licence in the 16th century and bowling greens were permitted at inns in 1688.

Solihull Bowling Green at the *George Hotel* appears to be very ancient and was possibly made in 1693 when Dog Lane Croft was acquired. A large yew tree estimated by botanists to be about 600 years old is situated to one side of the green and has been trained into an arbour, giving a view of the green and space for 12 people. A topiary peacock sat on top of the arbour but became rather neglected by the 1980s—restoration work is attempting to improve matters.

The earliest mention of the bowling green occurs in the *Gentleman's Magazine* of August 1790 when the death of William James was reported. Mr. James was described as 'assistant to the Bowling Green at Solihull' and had died following a sudden illness (possibly pneumonia). It was also reported that his pall bearers fulfilled his last request that they play a game of bowls after the funeral.

A report appeared in the *St James Chronicle* (a national newspaper) in 1791 recording a public argument between the Rev. Charles Curtis and the Rev. Dr. Samuel Parr, Vicar of Hatton, at an event at the bowling green the previous year. Curtis was a Tory and Parr supported the Whigs so there were long-standing differences of opinion. Dr. Parr had received anonymous letters and accused Mr. Curtis of sending them, which sparked the notorious altercation at the green. The Rev. James Eyre (then Headmaster of Solihull Grammar School) and Dr. Ward from Coventry attempted to intervene between the two but with little success.

Although this dispute may now appear ridiculous, it must be seen in the context of the times. Tories were usually Anglican and conservative while Whigs were often Dissenters such as Quakers or Unitarians and free-thinking liberals, which led to suspicions of sympathy with revolutionary ideas. In nearby Birmingham the paranoia following the French Revolution led to the 'Priestley Riots' in 1791 when the homes of Joseph Priestley and most of the prominent non-conformists were destroyed. As Rector of Birmingham, Curtis was a magistrate there and Parr was related to Joseph Priestley by marriage. One wonders what Sir William Curtis, Lord Mayor of London in 1798, made of his brother's notoriety.

Archer Clive succeeded Charles Curtis and often attended the bowling club to play at bowls (sometimes late in the evening after it became dark) and to have dinner. On 14 September 1842 Archer recorded in his diary,[7] 'Wednesday, what my wife [Caroline] in her pride calls "pig and pearl" day, I being the pearl and the other members of the Bowling Green the pigs. After all we had a tolerably merry evening, bowls, dinner and whist.'

Solihull Bowling Club continues to meet at the bowling green behind the *George Hotel* and has several trophies, the earliest being presented by Joseph Hillman (proprietor of the *George*) in May 1896.

Solihull Cricket Club was founded in the 1850s and the Football Club followed later in 1891. Both clubs used land at Broomfields near the Union Workhouse. A cycling club appears to have existed at the end of the 19th century, although little information has survived. A membership booklet dated 1893 for Solihull Bicycle Club with its headquarters at Knowle still existed in 1985 and contained a programme of events; Cycling Club programmes appeared in the *Parish Magazine* in the early 1900s. Photographs of groups of cyclists allegedly dating from 1887 and 1891 were published in the *Solihull News* in 1979. The first group included Sir Alfred Bird, who moved to live in Solihull in 1901, and the second shows George and Ernest Powell and local artists Oswald and Raphael Pippet, apparently touring in France.

Solihull Cycling Club was founded in 1929 by Eric Walker, Tommy Hawks, Ivor Goodman and Arthur Houlston. Mr. Hawks worked for Captain Oliver Bird (son of Sir Alfred) as a chauffeur and was an experienced cyclist. The other founder members were local teenagers living in Catherine-de-Barnes.

The inaugural meeting was held on 13 February 1929 when Mr. A. Logan was elected

150 Solihull Football Club, first team, with Dr. Whitehouse (*centre*), 1921.

Chairman and Victor Pegg (owner of a cycle shop in Solihull) Secretary. Unusually at that time, the club was open to men and women. Happily, the club continues today with a flourishing membership and a varied programme.

Many national events have been celebrated in the town, including the Coronation of Queen Victoria on 28 June 1838. The weather was pleasantly warm and sunny. A special service was held in St Alphege Church, when Archer Clive preached a sermon based on a text from the *Book of Kings*, 'And Judah and Israel dwelt safely every man under his vine and under his fig tree' (presumably a hope for peace and prosperity in the new reign).

The Sunday School children were given medals commemorating the event and a dinner was then given to the poor, served by the local gentry, principal farmers and trades people in a tent in the Square made of tarpaulins decorated with evergreens and flowers. The diners sat at three rows of tables and the menu consisted of

151 The Fire Brigade and procession celebrating Queen Victoria's Diamond Jubilee, 1897.

152 High Street decorated for the Coronation of King George V, 1911.

beef, bread, potatoes, plum pudding, beer and ale. Shirley residents received a similar dinner and the total cost of £89 was raised by public subscription. The local band was in attendance and played the national anthem after the loyal toast had been proposed by the Rector.

Queen Victoria enjoyed a very long reign and her Golden and Diamond Jubilees in 1887 and 1897 were celebrated in the town with much style. Special services were held in St Alphege Church followed by processions of local organisations, sports events and teas. The town was decorated on both occasions with bunting, flags and huge floral arches. In 1887 Malvern Park was opened by permission of Herbert Bainbridge, who was the tenant of Malvern Hall at the time. Sports and amusements 'for young and old' included a merry-go-round and shooting gallery. Children were given a commemorative medal and a Jubilee mug. It was estimated that 5,000 people visited Solihull that day. In 1887 an oak tree was planted at the junction of Streetsbrook Road and Station Road, and a stone was added in 1897 recording the event. The Jubilee Stone was moved into Station Road when the traffic island was created c.1967.

In June 1900, during the Boer War, the news that Pretoria had been taken by British troops was celebrated with processions through Solihull.

The town band played patriotic songs and townsfolk were joined by boys from Solihull School. Some of the boys had decorated their bicycles with flags and ribbons for the occasion and the day concluded with a bonfire.

The Coronation of Edward VII had been planned for 26 June 1902 but the King was taken ill with appendicitis and the ceremony was postponed, although an announcement from Buckingham Palace indicated that events should take place as planned. Some events in Solihull went ahead, including a dinner and children's tea in Malvern Park, but the sports events, bonfire and firework display were postponed. The King made a remarkable recovery from his operation

153 Pensioners celebrating the Coronation of Queen Elizabeth II, 1953.

154 Unknown wedding, *c*.1910.

155 Unknown wedding reception.

and was crowned on 9 August. There had been much concern over the King's health before the ceremony but ironically it was the Archbishop of Canterbury, not the King, who was taken ill during the proceedings.

King George V and Queen Mary were crowned on 22 June 1911 and once again Solihull town centre was decorated with flags and bunting and elaborate floral arches were erected in the High Street, Warwick Road and Park Road. Poulter's stationer's advertised 'coloured papers, streamers and Coronation serviettes for your table'. Dr. Bernays (or his chauffeur) even decorated his motor car. The customary service was held in St Alphege Church, as prescribed by the Archbishop of Canterbury, and there was a procession around the town. Sports were held for the local children, there were Maypole dancing and folk songs, and a tea when each child was presented with a commemorative mug.

George V lived to celebrate his Silver Jubilee in May 1935, when there were festivities in the area. Jubilee Park in Olton was named in honour of the event. George died in 1936 and was succeeded by his eldest son Edward VIII, who abdicated in favour of his younger brother

following a crisis caused by his attachment to American divorcee Wallis Simpson.

Consequently the next major celebration was the Coronation of George VI on 12 May 1937. A special service was held in St Alphege Church and an extensive programme of events at Shirley included a pageant, fancy dress and piano accordion competitions, community singing, a torchlight procession, a bonfire and a firework display.

Many events were held during the Second World War to raise money for the war effort and raise morale. However the main celebrations were reserved until 1945 when VE and VJ Days marked the end of hostilities in Europe and the Far East. In spite of rationing and food shortages local residents managed to hold street parties.

Celebrations were held in honour of the Coronation of Queen Elizabeth II in 1953 and for the Silver Jubilee in 1977, when the Queen visited Solihull.

Countless generations of Silhillians have held private celebrations to mark weddings and other family occasions. Fortunately some of these have been recorded by local photographers such as Arthur Hobbins (who probably recorded the bride shown here), Edwin and Hugh Trinder, David Jewsbury and Cliff Joiner.

Nine

Solihull in Wartime

Although the global wars of the 20th century had the greatest impact on the civilian population, earlier conflicts and invasions also affected every-day life. The local Celtic farmers had to come to terms with the invaders from Rome in the 1st century AD and four hundred years later new compromises were necessary to cope with the invasions of the Angles and Saxons. Some doubt-less accepted the new settlers and intermarried while others held out against the invaders and were eventually pushed west into Wales. In the 11th century a new order came with the Norman conquerors, although, as noted in Chapter One, both the local manors of Ulverlei and Longdon still had Saxon lords in 1086.

By the end of 1086 Ulverlei was granted by William I to Ralph de Limesi and eventually passed to Hugh de Oddingsell by his marriage to Basilia de Limesi. Hugh was a soldier and described by William Dugdale[1] as an important person. He supported King Henry III in person at the siege of Bitham Castle in Lincolnshire *c*.1220. His son William also fought for Henry III and, according to Dugdale, 'this William [was] attendant upon the King, in person, beyond the Seas'. Later described as a '*miles strenus*' (a keen soldier), he was made Governor of Montgomery Castle.

William bequeathed Ulverlei to his younger son, another William, who supported the King in Wales and Ireland and was knighted in 1283. Men from Solihull could have accompanied their lords on all these and later campaigns.

The manor of Solihull was granted to Edward, Duke of York in 1414 but a year later he was killed at the Battle of Agincourt. Men were obliged to practise archery at the butts in order to retain the skills necessary for warfare should they be required to follow their king into battle. Marks are still visible on the west wall of St Alphege Church where arrows were sharpened on the stones.

The various civil wars would have had some impact for residents of Solihull, although no major battles were fought in the immediate vicinity. Local men continued to enlist at times of national emergencies. Joseph Swinburne was a notable figure, who was born in Solihull in 1783 and enlisted in the 83rd Regiment of Foot around 1809 at the time of the Peninsular War. He served in Portugal, Spain and France, fighting in major battles including Talavera, Badajoz and Salamanca. He so distinguished himself that he was promoted from the ranks and eventually in 1851 gained the rank of Colonel when serving in India, possibly the first to rise from private to colonel. After the defeat of Napoleon Joseph also served with his regiment in Canada and Ceylon. If all this sounds familiar, it may be because Joseph's fictional 'double', Richard Sharpe, springs to mind. Joseph died at Lichfield in 1860 aged 76 and was buried in Solihull Church, where a memorial tablet in the chancel records some of his achievements.

The Napoleonic wars brought a real threat of invasion to Britain for the first time since the Spanish Armada set sail. To offset this threat local units of militia were created as an 18th-century version of the Home Guard and every parish had to supply men—Solihull was required to provide seven. The Rev. Charles Curtis and other leading residents, such as members of the Harding and Chattock families, decided to do more and founded a volunteer Troop of Horse, containing 38 members who provided their horses and uniforms at their own expense.

West's Directory of Warwickshire for 1830 records that Henry Greswolde Lewis of Malvern Hall erected a wooden obelisk to commemorate Napoleon's final defeat in 1815 at the Battle of Waterloo. The obelisk was described as being about 180 feet high, painted white and enclosed by a railing supported by the trunks of 'venerable' trees with an inscription to the 'brave British

156 The Rev. C.O.R. Wormald, Vicar of Shirley 1913-7, Rector of Solihull 1926-35.

At the beginning of the First World War in September 1914 Solihull was little more than a village surrounded by country lanes and farmland and with new houses in roads such as Ashleigh Road and Whitefields Road. Many men were employed in agriculture or related occupations while others worked in business or a profession in Birmingham.

Lord Kitchener issued his famous 'Call to Arms' urging men between the ages of 19 and 30 to enlist. The Rector of Solihull, the Rev. T.B. Harvey Brooks, added his encouragement in an article published in *Solihull Parish Magazine* in September 1914. He wrote,

> Everyone is wanted. To every able bodied man comes the call to arms and to everybody else comes the call to service at home. We can use self-denial in expenditure on food, comfort and amusement and be ready to give our money and our time and our services in helping the sick and wounded and all to whom war brings poverty and distress.

Many young men from Solihull heeded the call, including the Rector's son-in-law, the Rev. Charles Wormald, who was then Vicar of Shirley and later succeeded Harvey Brooks as Rector of Solihull. Another was Walter Wilsdon (son of James, the founder of Wilsdon & Co) who saw action with the Royal Artillery at Ypres, Arras and the Somme before returning home to take over the family business. A few photographs survive showing soldiers or sailors with their families or friends before their departure overseas. Even fewer photographs show them on their return.

For the families left behind there followed an agonising wait for news. Telegrams were often sent to inform relatives of casualties. A telegram sent to Mrs. E. Jacobs in Whitefields Road, Solihull, on 21 July 1918 survives—its message was short and to the point: 'Deeply regret to inform you Captain R Jacobs RAMC Died of Wounds 20th July. Army Council express their sympathy'. The family later received an illuminated scroll and letter signed by King George V recording Robert Jacobs' sacrifice. The family also requested the War Office to send a photograph of his grave at the cemetery in Avesnes-le-Comte. These items are now deposited in Solihull Library.

Older men were left to carry on the agriculture in the area, sometimes assisted by land

army and their Allies'. Geoffrey Martineau also mentioned the obelisk, stating that it stood at the far end of the avenue at Malvern Hall (now Brueton Avenue), not on Warwick Road but on Hampton Lane near Ivy Hall. He said, 'This was made of wood, so has not lasted very long, and had disappeared before any houses were built there'. No other record of the obelisk exists.

Local men saw action in the Crimean and the Boer Wars. In January 1900 the Parish Magazine recorded that five local Reservists (Mr. Clarke, William Green, William White, Arthur Hobbins and George Florence) had joined their regiment in London. William Green was later invalided home from South Africa. At least 19 other men from Solihull enlisted and fought in the war and memorials have been erected to some, for example, the tablet in Solihull Church in memory of Private John T. Johnson, who died at Maritzburg, South Africa in 1900. The Parish Magazine published letters sent home by Charles Blake and Harry Cheadle but surprisingly did not mention the end of the war.

157 Members of the Harrison family with an unknown rifleman.

158 Members of the Edginton family at the wedding of an unknown trooper.

159   War widow Mrs. Harriet Davis from Drury Lane, with Blanche and John.

girls such as Ida Markham from Whar Hall Farm. Further opportunities for women began to emerge as shortages of workers were experienced, including jobs such as delivering bread for Cooper's Bakery in Olton.

Other women joined the Red Cross to train as nurses. Some were sent abroad to help nurse servicemen too ill or injured to travel, while others nursed convalescent soldiers in the Solihull area.

Several large houses in the Solihull district were converted into temporary hospitals for the use of wounded servicemen. 'The Hermitage' in Lode Lane was such a hospital: in four and a half years 2,122 patients were treated there by the Commandant, Miss Townshend, and her staff. Dr. Whitehouse from Warwick Road, Solihull, was in charge of the hospital. Local residents often sent gifts of fruit or food to the patients. As the men recovered, those able to walk could sometimes be seen in the town, wearing their special uniforms of light blue jackets and trousers with a red tie.

Many houses in the neighbourhood of Solihull were used for Red Cross hospitals including 'The Rookery' in St Bernard's Road, Olton, Springfield House in Knowle, the Fentham Institute in Hampton-in-Arden and the Rectory

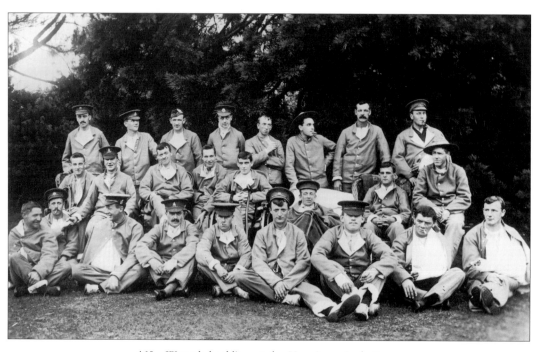

160   Wounded soldiers at the Hermitage, Lode Lane.

161 Dedication of the War Memorial, 19 June 1921.

at Berkswell. Doris Hamilton Smith was typical of the many local girls helping the Red Cross. Doris helped at the Hermitage and received a certificate at the end of the war. There was little direct action against civilians in the Solihull area, although bombs were dropped by Zeppelin airships at Packwood Haugh School and in a field behind the *Red Lion* in Shirley.

In July 1919 a national celebration called Peace Day was held to mark the end of the War. Photographs survive showing activities at Shirley and Bickenhill. For bereaved families, such as Mr. and Mrs. Geoffrey Martineau of Touchwood Hall who lost their son Clement and Mrs. Davis (their neighbour in Drury Lane) who was left a widow with two young children, there was little comfort in these festivities.

After the War it was decided to erect a War Memorial in the centre of the Square to commemorate those who did not return to Solihull. The memorial was designed by the architect W.H. Bidlake and was unveiled by the Earl of Craven in a solemn service on 19 June 1921. The Bishop of Birmingham dedicated the Memorial, Dr. Adolphus Bernays read the names of the fallen, a firing party fired three volleys and the 'Last Post' was sounded. The names of those killed in the Second World War and the Korean War have since been added to the Memorial, which was moved to the side of the Square near the churchyard wall in 1994.

Solihull Congregational Church made its own Roll of Honour, recording its 41 members who had served their country and the six who had lost their lives. The list includes several relatives. Other churches in the area erected memorials naming members of their congregations who had lost their lives.

At the outbreak of the Second World War in September 1939 Solihull had been an Urban District Council (UDC) for a little more than five years. The new Council House in Poplar Road had been open since 1937 and became the co-ordination centre for the District, with operations directed from a command centre in the basement.

Mr. Roy Townsend remembered[2] that the Operations Room was constructed so that it ran

162   Barrage balloon team at Lode Heath School.

the full length of the basement (which had been reinforced with steel girders). The Command Centre was staffed 24 hours a day. A team of five Council Staff were on duty from 9.00 a.m. to 5.00 p.m. and staff were expected to work a night shift every third week. Volunteers worked in the evenings from 6.00p.m. to 10.00p.m. The Controller sat at the head table and several telephones on a long table provided links to the emergency services and to Superintendents of Council services at home. Charles Hutchinson, the Engineer & Surveyor of the UDC, was the Chief of the Command Centre. An Observation Box was also built on the roof of the Council House. This consisted of a box about three feet wide by five feet long where two people at a time took turns to keep watch.

Barrage balloons appeared throughout the District and searchlight batteries were erected. Several smoke screens were put in place in Solihull and other villages around Birmingham. The smoke screens were created by setting fire to large drums of crude oil which produced clouds of acrid smelling smoke intended to confuse enemy planes and reduce attacks on Birmingham.

Identity cards were issued and new rules and regulations were introduced especially from the Air Raid Precautions (ARP). Many of these remained clear in residents' memories for decades—the same phrases recur when people talk about the period: for example 'not a chink of light must show' (that is from the outside) when the blackout curtains were closed.

Air-raid shelters were hastily erected in 1939. Public shelters were constructed in the street, for example in Warwick Road or at public buildings, and individual shelters were built in many gardens. The government issued 'Anderson' shelters for use outside and 'Morrison' table shelters for indoor use. Shelters were supplied in parts with instruction booklets. An air-raid siren was situated on the roof of Solihull Fire Station in Streetsbrook Road.

Although at first it was feared that there would be many air raids, especially in view of the proximity of Birmingham, Solihull actually suffered few raids. There were some attacks, however, such as an early morning raid on Solihull High Street which damaged Winfield's chemists' shop and destroyed Duddy's wool

shop. The same plane also attempted to bomb
Solihull Gas Works but hit houses in Alston
Road and Cornyx Lane in the process. Several
people were killed or injured and one entire
family was killed. Shirley and Olton also experienced some raids.

In case of gas attacks residents were also issued
with gas masks which were to be carried at all
times. All were encouraged to test their gas masks
and to practise using them in a room filled with
tear gas. There was a facility available at Solihull
Gas Works.

Children from Solihull were not evacuated
to other areas as it did not become a high risk for
air raids. Solihull became a reception area for
evacuees, first from the East End of London and
later from Coventry.

Many men between the ages of 18 and 40
were away with the armed forces, but some older
and younger men remained together with those
in reserved occupations doing jobs essential for
the war effort. Solihull UDC adopted a 'V/W'
class destroyer called HMS *Vivacious* in 1942 and
the crew were supported with gifts and comforts
sent from local people. A group of officers and
other ranks visited the town for a weekend in
March 1944 at the invitation of the UDC. The
guests were entertained with events including a
reception, a dance and a football match between
a team from the ship and a team from the UDC
workers. HMS *Vivacious* had been built at Yarrow

163 Mr. and Mr. Robinson's wedding, 24 April
1943.

164 Entertaining the
crew of HMS *Vivacious* in
the Public Hall, March
1944.

165   Mrs. Herraty inspecting components at the Rover Aero Factory.

in 1917 and happily survived the War, eventually being sold in 1947.

Several factories were located in the Solihull area including the Rover 'Shadow' factory in Lode Lane, the Austin Aero Works near Elmdon Airport and the BSA in Shirley. The Rover factory 'shadowed' production at its factory in Acocks Green, so that components would still be produced if the other factory were damaged or destroyed.

Rolls Royce engines for Hercules and Lancaster bombers were produced at the Rover factory, where many of the workers were women who had been conscripted for war work. Much of the work was dirty and exacting. Mrs. Herraty remembered[3] inspecting engines 'dripping with oil' for cracks or damage made in testing—workers had to sit on high stools standing on duck boards to keep their feet out of the oil while this was done, but they still suffered dermatitis from the oil and tinnitus from the constant noise.

The Austin Aero Works was situated on the site later occupied by the Elmdon Trading Estate and assembled aeroplanes from parts made at the Austin factory in Longbridge. Short Stirling bombers were made first, followed from around 1943 by Lancaster bombers. Completed planes were towed along a path which crossed the railway to be tested at Elmdon Airport (later Birmingham International Airport). Elmdon was also used to train pilots during the War.

Other essential jobs included water, gas and electricity supply and emergency repairs after air raids. The gas workers were particularly at risk when attending a severed gas main. Solihull Fire Station served a wide area and men from Solihull were reported at the disastrous fire which destroyed Coventry Cathedral on 14 November 1940.

Many men in essential jobs joined the Home Guard or the ARP and young men under eighteen often joined the Cadets or the Air Training Corps to begin training. Women too joined in activities such as fire watching or first aid or joined the Girls Training Corps or Women's Land Army.

166   Short Stirling bomber at Austin Aero works at Elmdon.

For civilians Solihull had only a cottage hospital (which had formerly been the Infirmary of the Union Workhouse) at the outbreak of War. This became an Emergency Hospital but had inadequate facilities. Paul Quinet, a local surgeon, recorded in his autobiography that he used his own portable X-ray machine there. In addition to routine medical care, injuries caused by air raids or (more often) by accidents happening in the blackout were treated there.

Some military hospitals were also created for the care and nursing of wounded soldiers, including an Auxiliary Hospital staffed by the British Red Cross Association with beds for 50

167   Home Guard at the Rover works, 1941.

168   Roy Townsend (*in plane*) at No.41 Elementary Gliding School, Knowle.

convalescent patients at 'Tudor Grange' in Blossomfield Road. The house is now (2001) part of Solihull College but was then the home of the Dowager Lady [Eleanor] Bird, widow of Sir Alfred Bird whose father invented Bird's Custard Powder. Another Auxiliary Hospital was set up at a house called 'Totehill' in Blossomfield Road where 25 patients could be treated. Paul Quinet was Medical Officer of Health for both hospitals and the matrons were Mrs. Wainwright and Mrs. Thompson. Princess Mary (the Princess Royal) visited the hospitals in 1944. 'Totehill' became the headquarters of the Red Cross in Solihull after the war and continued in use until the late 1990s.

Obtaining food was a national preoccupation. Rationing was introduced, allowing very small amounts of butter or margarine, cheese, meat and sugar per person. It was necessary to register with a butcher or grocer and then use only that shop. Coupons had to be surrendered at the time of purchase and shopkeepers had to return the coupons to the Food Office in Warwick Road each week. Rationing also covered clothes and

furniture. It was often a case of 'make do and mend'.

Most factories had a canteen where workers could obtain a nourishing (if plain) meal. A chain of 'British Restaurants' was established where a reasonably priced meal could be purchased by schoolchildren or those with no access to a works canteen. Meals were nourishing and wholesome and made from whatever ingredients were available on a given day. An average price was a shilling for a main course. The 'British Restaurant' in Solihull was situated in Mill Lane in the former Boys' School.

Residents were encouraged to grow vegetables to supplement rations and to help reduce the amount of food imported, as convoys of ships were at great risk from enemy action and required protection from the Navy. Most gardens and many local schools and employers turned over any available land for the use of pupils and employees. Pupils at Salter Street School were recorded growing vegetables and land was available at Solihull Gas Works. Many people kept a few chickens for eggs and meat or a pig (which had to be registered).

169 Opening of the British Restaurant in former Mill Lane School, 13 June 1942.

A number of farms and smallholdings remained in the Solihull area at the end of the 1930s and as much land as possible was used to produce food. As the War dragged on prisoners of war began to appear. Some German prisoners helped to grow vegetables in Dorchester Road and Italians worked in Damson Lane.

Eventually food parcels arrived, sometimes from relatives living abroad. Various organisations in the USA sent parcels including CARE (Co-operative for American Remittances to Europe) which was partly organised by the actor Douglas Fairbanks Jnr. A celebration attended by Mr. Fairbanks and Solihull dignitaries was held at the Commonwealth Gift Centre in London in July 1949.

Local entertainment was limited and there were many privations to be endured but in spite of (or perhaps because of) this there was a spirit of comradeship. Going to see a film was very popular and programmes often changed twice a week. There were cinemas in Solihull High Street, Olton and Shirley. There were many public houses in the area and there were

170 Exhibition in London celebrating American aid: *left to right* Martin Lindsay MP, Councillor M. Walker and Douglas Fairbanks Jnr., 1949.

occasional dances. Many social events were held which were linked to one of the many fund raising events such as 'Salute a Soldier Week', 'Wings for Victory' and 'Dig for Victory'. However, with so many families separated by the War and so few opportunities for travel,

171 Wilbur Matheson (*left*) and John Werthman from US Army visiting Dorchester Road.

time dragged by and boredom and tedium became a problem.

Transport was difficult; petrol was rationed and non-essential vehicles were prohibited. Many private cars were laid up for the duration of the War either at home or at a local garage, and with the rotor arm removed to prevent their use by the enemy in the case of an invasion. Buses ran to Birmingham when conditions in the city permitted but the last bus returned to Solihull at about 9.00p.m. Many people used bicycles, but it was difficult to ride at night in the blackout as

there were no streetlights and traffic lights were masked so that only a small cross of light showed. It was impossible to obtain batteries for cycle lamps, but some cyclists had a dynamo although great care had to be taken to mask the lights.

Motor garages such as 'Solihull Motors' were commissioned by the Ministry of Defence to refurbish and maintain the vehicles necessary for communications in Britain. It was impossible to obtain new cars (or often even to buy spare parts) because car factories such as Rover were given over to munitions work. Staff at the garage would

172 VJ Party in Ulleries Road, Olton, August 1945.

collect worn out or faulty cars from far afield and tow them back to Solihull in convoys to refurbish or cannibalise for spare parts, if the vehicle had gone too far for restoration.

When the USA joined the War many American servicemen were sent to Britain to train for the invasion of Europe which was to begin with the 'D' Day landings in Normandy in 1944. An American Army Headquarters was created in Blossomfield Road, Solihull, on the site later occupied by Tudor Grange Swimming Baths. Some soldiers were in a camp at Catherine-de-Barnes while others were billeted with local families, two and three at a time.

Many of the GIs were themselves little more than boys and were away from home for the first time. Some made friendships which lasted for decades. Mr. James S. Jones from the US Military Police remembered[4] arriving at Solihull in a blacked-out train after a long journey from Scotland, where their ship had landed in the Firth of Clyde. He recalled drinking 'warm' beer in the village pubs and attending a show put on by

local residents to entertain the Americans—the Chairman of the UDC made a speech which was valued by the visitors. He also remembered visiting a family in Dorchester Road, where he was treated as an honoured guest. Mr. Lloyd Sweet from the US Army recalled[5] visiting the same family, spending evenings in conversation and joining them in church.

Many people remember the Americans, especially local children who often greeted the men with catch phrases such as 'Got any gum, chum?'. The Americans often shared their generous sweet rations with the children. Many recall the sudden mobilisation prior to 'D' Day when convoy after convoy drove through the town and disappeared.

When victory in Europe came, it was greeted with much joy and celebration on VE Day on 8 May 1945. In spite of rationing and other limitations most streets or villages managed to arrange a party with food—at least for the children—and games. More celebrations followed in August on VJ (Victory in Japan) Day.

Ten

Epilogue

By 1950 Solihull had begun its metamorphosis from small country town to suburbia. Urban District status in 1932 had been an indication of future development but the creation of the Municipal Borough in 1954 led to dramatic changes and the elevation to County Borough in 1964 paved the way to expansion. Each rise in local government status gave greater powers to the Council and reflected the growing population.

Housing developments slowly engulfed the farmland surrounding the town. New roads were created for the estates, which also required schools, shops, doctors' surgeries, community centres and public houses.

More shops were built in the town centre when the Mell Square development was constructed in the 1960s in collaboration with Norwich Union and this was extended when Poplar Way was added in 1975.

Work on a civic centre commenced with the Civic Hall in 1962, followed in 1968 by a new Council House and Civic Suite Chamber; the Central Library and Theatre opened in 1976.

Sports facilities including tennis courts, swimming baths, an athletics centre and an all weather running track were created alongside the town's three parks, Malvern Park, Brueton Park and Tudor Grange Park.

In 1974 Solihull became a Metropolitan Borough (SMBC) and this change brought much greater responsibility as the new Borough is much larger than its predecessors. More staff were needed to carry out all the statutory functions and the council became one of the largest local employers. In 1989 an extension was built to enlarge the Council House.

In the 1980-90s a 'mini town' was built on former farmland and countryside between Solihull and Monkspath, south of Shirley. Approximately 10,000 houses were built there in little more than eight years. The development included public open space, a business park, and a small shopping centre with a community centre, school and public house (created out of Shelly Farmhouse and its barn).

At the same time commercial development was taking place in the town centre creating new offices and hotels. Several large companies relocated their head offices to prestigious new buildings.

In the late 1980s SMBC decided that the town centre required economic regeneration and the eventual outcome was the Touchwood shopping development (due to open in September 2001). This is the result of a partnership between Lendlease and John Lewis and will provide a department store, shops, restaurants and a cinema, creating hundreds of new jobs in the process.

Business and commercial developments take advantage of Solihull's position at the heart of Britain's motorway and rail networks. Birmingham International Airport is situated two miles to the north and offers excellent regional and international transport. It can therefore be said that Solihull has returned to its original position as a thriving commercial centre taking advantage of contemporary communications networks although the present town is a far cry from the market town created in the 12th century.

Notes

Chapter One
1. Skipp, V., *The Origins of Solihull* (1964), p.13.
2. Skipp, V., *The Origins of Solihull* (1964), p.1.
3. Dugdale, W., *The Antiquities of Warwick* (1656).
4. Skipp, V., *The Origins of Solihull* (1964), p.8.
5. van Wart, I., *Souvenir of Old England* (1880), p.8.
6. Martineau, G., *Solihull from 1863 and onwards* (1933).
7. Wedge, J., *A General View of Agriculture in Warwickshire* (1794).

Chapter Two
1. van Wart, I., *Souvenir of Old England* (1880), p.5.
2. Clive, Archer and Caroline *MS Diaries* (1838-47) [microfilm].
3. Martineau, G., *Solihull from 1863 and onwards* (1933).
4. Stewart, E., [*MS memories*] (1981) filed in Solihull Library.
5. Hatton, W., [*MS memories*] (1999) filed in Solihull Library.
6. Gorton, Mrs., [*MS memories*] (1988) filed in Solihull Library.
7. Martineau, G., *Solihull from 1863 and onwards* (1933).

Chapter Three
1. Martineau, G., *Solihull from 1863 and onwards* (1933).
2. Clive, Archer and Caroline *Ms Diaries* (1838-47) [microfilm].
3. Martineau, G., *Solihull from 1863 and onwards* (1933).
4. Boston, Noel, *Solihull and the surrounding district* (1929).

Chapter Four
1. *Solihull Parish Magazine* Jan-Mar 1940.

Chapter Five
1. Martineau, G., *Solihull from 1863 and onwards* (1933).
2. Burman, J., *Solihull and its School* (1949), p.65.
3. van Wart, I., *Souvenir of old England* (1880), p.39.

Chapter Six
1. Smith, E. Orford, *1872-9: Seven Years Work of a Rural Sanitary Authority* (1879).
2. Martineau, G., *Solihull from 1863 and onwards* (1933).

Chapter Seven
1. van Wart, I., *Souvenir of Old England* (1880), p.28.
2. Wilson, W., *Green Peas at Christmas* (1924).
3. van Wart, I., *Souvenir of Old England* (1880), pp.14-5.

Chapter Eight
1. Lines, Charles, 'Shops in the High Street' (*Solihull News*, 3 March 1973).
2. Lines, Charles, *Britain in Old Photographs: Solihull* (1998), p.19.
3. van Wart, I., *Souvenir of Old England* (1880), p.6.
4. Clive, Archer and Caroline *MS Diaries* (1838-47) [microfilm].
5. Clive, Archer and Caroline *MS Diaries* (1838-47) [microfilm].
6. Wilson,W., *Green Peas at Christmas* (1924).
7. Clive, Archer and Caroline *MS Diaries* (1838-47) [microfilm].

Chapter Nine
1. Dugdale,W., *Antiquities of Warwickshire* (1656).
2. Bates, S. (editor), *Solihull in Wartime (1939-45)* (1995), pp.71-2.
3. Bates, S. (editor), *Solihull in Wartime (1939-45)* (1995) pp.43-4.
4. Bates, S. (editor), *Solihull in Wartime (1939-45)* (1995), pp.65-6.
5. Bates, S. (editor), *Solihull in Wartime (1939-45)* (1995), p.67.

Bibliography

Bates, Sue, *Shirley: A Pictorial History* (1993)

Bates, Sue, *Solihull: A Pictorial History* (1991)

Bates, Sue (ed.), *Solihull in Wartime* (1995)

Bates, Sue, *Select list of Sources relating to Solihull in Solihull Local Studies Collection* (1999)

Birmingham University Extra Mural Department (series of unpublished research papers) (1970s)

Burman, J., *Solihull and its School* (1939 and 1949)

Caselton, S.H., *Solihull Bowling Club: A Brief History* (1991)

Clive, M., *Caroline Clive* (1949)

Davis, A., *The First 25 Years of the Daughter Church of St Francis of Assisi* (1975)

Edwards, E., 'The Medieval Market Town of Solihull' (MA Thesis 1992).

Guide to St Alphege Church (1989)

Handley, Edna, *Bentley Heath and Widney Manor* (1992)

Handley, Edna, *Travelling On: The Continuing Story of Methodism in Solihull* (1997)

Jones, R., *A Solihull Century* (1998)

Kelly's Directories of Warwickshire (1896, 1900, 1908, 1912, 1916, 1921, 1928, 1932, 1936, 1940)

Malley, Bernard, *Solihull and the Catholic Church* (1939)

Martineau, Geoffrey, *Reminiscences* (1930s)

Martineau, Philip, *A Short Guide to Solihull*, being the Substance of a Lecture Delivered before Solihull Science and Arts Association (1902)

Pemberton, R., *Solihull and its Church* (1905)

Pigot's Directories of Warwickshire (1822, 1842)

Quinet, D., *Paul Quinet* (1982)

St Helen's Church Centre—a new beginning (1974)

St Ninian's, Solihull—the first forty years (1986)

Sargent, C., *The History of Christchurch, Solihull* (1975)

Slater's Directory of Warwickshire (1862)

Skipp, Victor, *The Origins of Solihull* (1984)

Smith, E.O., *1872-9: Seven Years Work of a Rural Sanitary Authority* (1879)

Solihull Parish Magazine (1880-1958)

van Wart, Irving, *A Souvenir of Old England* (1880)

Victoria County History of Warwickshire, Volumes 1-6

Wager, Sarah J., *Woods, Wolds and Groves: the Woodland of Medieval Warwickshire* (1998)

West's Directory of Warwickshire (1830)

White's Directory of Warwickshire (1874)

Woodall, J., *The Book of Greater Solihull* (1990)

Woodall, J., *Gin and ale ... Solihull Workhouse and Hospital 1742-1993* (1993)

Woodall, J. and Varley, M., *Looking Back at Solihull* (1987)

Woodall, J. and Varley, M., *Solihull Placenames* (1979)

Index

References which relate to illustrations only are given in **bold**.

Addison, John, 8
Adult Education Centre, Blossomfield Road, 51
Air raids, 113, 114-5
Alder Brook, 2
Alderbrook Road, 64
Alderbrook School, 61
Alexander, Hilda, 49
Alice House, 64
Almar, 3
Alston, Squire, 98
Alston Road, 91, **93**, 115
Arden, Forest of, 2, 15, 72, 103
Ashleigh Road, **39**, **100**, 110
Austin Aero Works, 116, **117**
Aylesford, Earl of, 72

Baddesley Clinton, 67
Bainbridge, Herbert, 107
Balsall, 67
Balsall Common, 72
Bannister, George, 8
Barley Mow, **14**, 15, 16, 18, 32, 74, 103
Barratt, R.C., 51
Barston, 1, 2, 28, 67, 72
Beamond, John, 51
Becher Club, 100, 102
Beck, George, **12**
Bell, 103
Bentley Heath Mission Church, 44
Bentley Heath windmill, 25
Bentley Manor, 76
Berkswell, 72
Bernays, Adolphus, **39**, 40, 76, 77-8, **100**, 108, 113
Berry Hall: (new), 37, 74; (old), 7, 82
Bethesda Chapel, 48, 67
Bickenhill, 30, 72
Bidlake, W.H., 113
Bird, Sir Alfred, 91, 105, 118
Bird, Oliver, 45, 105
Bird, Lady Robert, 99
Birmingham International Airport, 72, 122
Birmingham Water Company, 73
Blake, Charles, 110
Blizzard sisters, 24
Blizzard's greengrocer's shop, 24

Blossomfield Farm, 7, 51
Blossomfield Road, **6**, 7, 91, 121
Blythe Bridge, **1**, **31**
Blythe, River, 1, 2, 27, 31, 67, 81
Boardman, R.G., 30
Boer War, 107, 110
Book Club, 97
Bourne's Seed Merchants, **22**
Bowling Club, **104**, 105
Brackley's Way, 45
Bradford House, 27
Bragg: Alfred, 21; Charles, 74; George, 23, 74; Grace, 102; Harvey, 21; Sarah, 57; Walter, 23
Bragg Brothers (builders), 21, 45
Bragg's butcher's shop, 21
Brickworks, 27
British Restaurant, 118, **119**
Broad Oaks Farm, 8
Broomfield, 27
Brueton, Horace, 89, 96-7
Brueton Avenue, 96, 110
Brueton Gardens, 89
Brueton Park, **97**, 122
Bull, Zelie, 64
Bullivant, John, 19
Burd, Charles, 37, 63
Burd, Marion, 63
Buryfield Road, 46, 61, 70
Bushwood, 67, 68
Byron, Lady 8

Caledonian Corks, 100
Carbis, William, 76, **77**
Carnival, **101**, 102
Cartland, Kathleen, 63
Castle Bromwich, 72
Castle Lane, 4
Catherine-de-Barnes, 67
Catherine-de-Barnes Heath, 2
Catherine-de-Barnes Mission Church, 44
Cattell: John 8; Joseph, 8
Cedarhurst Preparatory School, 64
Chambers, Samuel, 8
Chard, Alfred, 69
Charter Day, 70
Chattock family: 34, 109; Harvey, **77**; Richard, 65; Thomas, 104
Chatwin, J.A., 53

Cheadle, Harry, 110
Chelmsley Wood, 72
Cheltondale Road, 46
Christ Church, 49
Christadelphian Church, 51
Church Hill, 5, 6, 29, 46, 61, 86, 91, 95
Church House, **28**, 98
Church View, **90**
Churchill, Winston, 70
Church of Jesus Christ of Latter Day Saints, 27, 51
Cinemas, 119
Circuses, 95
Citizens' Advice Bureau, 86
City of Birmingham Electric Supply Department, 74
Civic centre car park, 25
Civic Hall, 70-1, 122
Clive: Archer, 16, 33, 42, 84-5, 96, 97, 105; Caroline, 16, 33, 34-5, 84-5, 96, 97-8, 104
Cole, River, 1
Colley's builders, **28**
Conference and Banqueting Centre, 25, 71
Congregational Church, 47-9, 113
Cook, Charles Herbert, 69
Cooke, E.A., 45
Cooke, Frances, 23
Cooper, A.J., 53
Cooper, R.D., 70
Coppice Road, 61
Coppice School, 61
Copt Heath, 2
Copt Heath Farm, 8
Copt Heath Windmill, 25
Cornyx Lane, 45, 91, 115
Couchman, Henry, 67
Couchman, R.H., 45, 46
Cow Hayes, 76
Cowrie, Dr, 96
Cran Brook, 2
Cranmore Boulevard, 30
Cricket Club, 105
Cristina, 3
Crompton, John, 55
Crook, Mrs, 63
Cull family, **90**
Currall, A.E., 67

Curtis, Charles, 48, 65, 83-4, 104, 105, 109
Cuttle Brook, 2
Cycling Club, 105-6

Dabridgecourt, Thomas, 53
Dame schools, 56
Damson Lane, 13, **34**, 119
Dascombe's pastrycook's shop, 24
Davis, Harriet, **112**, 113
De Feckenham, John, 47
De Limesi: family 4, 14, 41; Ralph, 109
De Oddingsell: Ela, 41; family 4, 15, 68; Hugh, 109; William, 5, 41, 109; William II, 41-2
Deebanks' shop, 24
Delmara, 63
Digby family, 72
Dilholme, 63
Dingle Lane, 64, 78
Dixon, Frank, 27
Doctor's House, 76, **78**
Dog Lane, 95
Dog Lane Croft, 105
Domesday Book, 2, 41
Dorchester Road, 119, **120**, 121
Dorridge, 34
Doughty, John, 8
Dovehouse Farm, **12**, 13, 82
Drury Lane, 19, 21, 23, 25, **28**, 32, 47-8, **72**, 80, 86, 89, 95, 98, 103, 104, 113
Duddy's wool shop, 114
Dugdale, William, 3, 109
Dunn, Reginald, 69
Dunstan Farm, 13

Earlswood Lakes, 1
Eastcote Brook, 2
Eborall, Cornelius, 23
Economic Water Softeners Ltd, 30
Edginton family, **111**
Edginton, Henry, 102
Edward VII: Coronation, 107
Edwards, George, 66
Edwards, Thomas, 23
Elizabeth II, 70, 107, 108
Elmdon, 67
Elmdon Airport, 116
Elmdon Hall, 98
Elmdon Hall Estate, 10, 13
Elmdon Heath, 2, 44, 47
Epsley & Co, 69
Evans, Mrs., 80, 99-100
Evans, Charles 80, 95, 97
Evans, Fanny, 86
Evans Convalescent Home, 80, 99-100
Eversfield School, 49, 64
Eyre, James, 105

Farming, 7-13
Feilding family, 75

Feldon, 2, 15
Findon, John, 28
Fire Service, 74-5, **106**
Fire Station, Streetsbrook Road, 75, 114
Fires, 75-6
First World War, 78, 89, 91, 110-3
Fisher, Elizabeth, 55
Florence, George, 110
Flower Show, **100**
Football Club, 105, **106**
Fordbridge, 72
Foredrove Farm, **11**, 13
Fossett's Circus, 95
Foster, Miss, 61
Fowgay Hall, 64, 78
Franklin, G.W., 13
Fraser, Edward, 44, 45
Freemasons, 100
Fripp, Joseph, **39**, 40, 78
Fulford Hall Road, 37

Gables, The, 24
Gardener's Arms, 103
Gateley, John, 103
George V: Coronation, **107**, 108; Silver Jubilee, 108
George VI: Coronation, 108
George, Charles, 27-8
George & Wilsdon, 28
George Hotel, 18, 32, **101**, 104, 105
Gillott: Joseph, 44, 56, 80; Maria, 44, 80
Glancey, Michael, 59
Golden End, 89
Golden Lion, 18, 102
Goodman, Ivor, 105
Gorton, Mrs., 24
Gospel Hall, Lode Lane, 51
Gospel Hall, Poplar Road, 51
Gough, John 8
Gould, William, 69
Grammar School, 52-5
Grand Union Canal, 32-3, **34**, 73
Grange Road, 75
Gray, Bertie, **35**
Great Western Railway, 33-4, **35**
Green, William, 110
Greswold family, 53, 59, 69, 72, 85
Greswolde Lewis, Henry, 84, 109
Greswolde Road, 61
Greswolde School, 61
Grove Road Clinic, 80

Hamilton Smith, Doris, 89, 113
Hampton Lane, 51, **81**, 110
Hampton-in-Arden, 72
Harborne, Thomas, 65
Harborne House, 86
Harbourn, Thomas, 21
Harold Cartwright School, 61
Harold Malley School, 61
Harris, William, 66, 67

Harrison family, **111**
Harvey Brooks, Ada Wynifred, 85
Harvey Brooks, T.B., **33**, **45**, 85, 96, 110
Hassall, Hugford, 47, 86
Hawes family, 53
Hawkes, Edward, 23
Hawks, Tommy, 105
Hayter, H.G., 38
Hazlewood, 89, **91**
Henry III, 5, 109
Henwood Hall, 46
Henwood Priory, 27, 46, 86
Henwood watermill, **26**, 27
Herbert Road, 24, 57, 89
Hermitage, 75, **76**, 112-3
Hermitage Road, 49, 91
High School for Girls, 59-61, 96
High Street, **15-7**, 18, 19, **20**, 21, **22**, 24-5, 29, **37-8**, 79, 85-6, 97, 108
Hillfield Farm, 13
Hillfield Hall, 9, 75
Hillman, Joseph, 105
Hobbins, Arthur, 23, 108, 110
Hobbins, Edward, 23
Hobbins' clockmaker's shop, 23
Hobs Moat, 3, 45
Hockley Heath, 71
Hodgkiss, James, 23
Holbeche family, 86
Holden, Edith, 40, 63
Holliday, James, 98
Homer, George, 44
Homer Road, 25, 27, 64, 89
Hood, William, 48
Hopkins, Charles, 98
Horne, Thomas, 86
Houlson, Arthur, 105
Howe, John, 66
Howman, John, 46-7
Hugford family, 53; Joan, 46; John, 46
Hull's butcher's shop, 24
Hurrell's Stores, 24
Hutchinson, C.R., 25, 114

Instone, Bernard, 30
Ivy Hall, 110

Jacobs, Robert, 110
Jago, Richard, 55
James, William, 105
Jasmine Lane, **93**
Jenkins, Roy, 70
Jewsbury, David, 108
Johnson: John, 69; John T., 110; Samuel, 55; William, **99**
Johnstone, James, 37
Joiner, Cliff, 108
Jubilee Park, 108
Jubilee Stone, 107

Ketelberne, 46
King, Laurence, 46

Kingshurst, 72
Knowle, 32, 33, 67

Land Rover, 30
Lane, Miss, 79
Lane, William, 79
Langstone Works, 30
Lapworth, 67, 68
Lea family: 82-3; Mary Ann, 21;
    Richard, 21; Walter, 21
Lea's grocer's shop, **20**, 21
Leal, James, 96
Leal's Annual Excursion, 96
Leal's draper's shop, 23
Ledbrook's Mews, **37**
Libbards House, 13, 83
Lifley, Emma, 86
Limerick Castle, 32
Lindsay: Joyce, **69**; Martin, **69**, 70,
    93, **119**
Lines: Annie, 29-30, 94; Charles, 30,
    94, 95; George, 29-30; Harold,
    30; William, 30
Literary Society, 98
Lode Heath, 2
Lode Heath School, 59, **114**
Lode Lane, 6, 9, 13, **25**, 30, 46, 63,
    75, 79, 89, **92**
Lode Lane industrial estate, 29
Logan, A., 105-6
London & Birmingham Railway, 33,
    34
Longdon, 3, 4, 14, 46, 109
Longdon Hall, 9
Lovekin, Alfred, 91
Lowe, Thomas, 76
Lugtrout Lane, **8**, 9
Luntley family, 82
Luxborough, Lady, 55

Madeley family: 27, 86; Caroline, 87;
    Charles, 27, 49, 67, 87; Ellen,
    87; Jessie, 87; Nellie, 87
Magistrates' Court, Warwick Road,
    89
Malley, Bernard, 47
Malt Shovel, 103
Malvern Hall, 37, 59-61, 84, 96,
    107, 110
Malvern House, **52**, 53
Malvern Park, 95, 96, 107, 122
Malvern Park Farm, **7**, 9, **10, 12**, 82
Malvern Park windmill, 25
Mann's Curio Shop, **17**, 19
Manor Farm, **13**
Manor House, 49, 85-6
Manor House Farm, 4, 13
Manor House Trust, 30
Margaret of Scotland, Saint, 3
Margaret, Princess, 70
Market, 5, 14, 15, 18
Markham, Bill, **10**
Markham, Ida, 112

Markham, John, **9**
Marshall Lake Road, 37
Marshall's ironmonger's shop, 23
Marston Green, 72
Martineau: Alfred, 87; Caroline, 6,
    79-80, 113; Clement, 87, 113;
    Geoffrey, 6, 18, 27, 32, 37, 53,
    55-6, 75, 79, 86-7, 110, 113
Martineau, Philip, 41
Mason's Arms, 103
Matthews family, 86, **96**
Matthews, George, 86
Medical Officer of Health, 66
Mell, W. Maurice, 25, **69**, 70
Mell Square, 25, 87, 122
Merevale Road, **28**
Meriden, 72
Meriden Constituency, 73
Meriden Rural District Council, 72
Meteor Works, 30
Methodist Church, 49-51
Mill Lane, 19, 23, 25, 56, 79, 89
Mill Lane Boys' School, 56, **58**, 59,
    118
Mills, Iain, 73
Moat Farm, 9
Moat House Hotel, 27
Moat Lane, 9
Monastery Drive, 51
Monkspath, 30, 122
Moore, Leslie, 45, 46
Morgan, H., **13**
Mothers' Union, **101**
Music Festival, 98

Nag's Head, 103
New Road, 19, 23, 56, 76
Nortmeade, 80
Norwich Union, 25, 122
Nuthurst, 67

Oak Cottage, 46
Oak Cottage School, 61
Oddfellows, 100, **101**
Odensil Farm, 13
Odeon Cinema, 70
O'Gorman, Mary, 57, 59
Old Lode Lane, 10, 27, **28**
Old Town Hall, 63, **65**, 89
Oliver Bird Hall, 59
Olton, 2, 4, 32, 33, 34, 40, 67
Olton Farm, 13
Olton Golf Course, 104
Olton Hall, 16, 46, 84, 104
Olton Mere, 33
Olton Tavern, 84
Olton Windmill, 25
Oxford & Birmingham Railway, 18,
    33-4, 44

Packhorse bridge, 31
Packwood, 67
Page, Edward Sutton, **36**, 76-7;

Erichsen, 77; Ferdinand, 77, **78**,
    86; Gilbert, 77; Shirley, 77
Palmer, Martha, 55, 56
Park Avenue, 97
Park Road, 28-9, 53, 63, **88**, 89,
    108
Park Road School, 53, 56-7
Parr, Samuel, 105
Peace Day, 113
Pearman: Ruth, 21; Susannah, 21;
    William, 21
Pegg, Victor, 106
Pemberton, Robert, 41
Pigstye hill, 5
Pippet family: 44; Elphege, 47;
    Gabriel, 47; Joseph, 47; Oswald,
    47, 105; Raphael, 105
Pitchford, Joe, 104
Pole, Edward, 52
Police Station, Homer Road, 25, 76;
    New Road, 76; Poplar Road,
    25, 76
Poplar House, 89
Poplar Way, 25, 122
Poplar Road, 23-4, 49, 70, 89
Population, 18
Post Office: Solihull 21, **37**; Shirley,
    21
Powell: Ernest, 105; George, 105;
    John, 61, 65
Powell's School, 61-3, 86
Priory, (new), 86,96; (old), 46, 61-3,
    86
Public Hall, 49, 51, 67, 98, **99**
Pugin, A.W.N., 47

Quinet: Doris, 76, 78-9; Paul, 76,
    78-9, 117, 118
Quinet House, 76

Radclyffe,T., 15
Railways, 18, 33-4
Ramsgate cottages, 73
Ravenshaw, 1, 76
Ravenshaw Hall, 81
Reading Room, 97, **98**
Rectory Estate, 91
Red Cross, 112, 117-8
Retselp Engineering, 30
Robin Hood Cemetery, 67-8
Robinson wedding, **115**
Roger's Garage, **40**
Rover Company, 30, 116, **117**
Rowood Farm, 13
Royal Oak Hotel, 38, 103
Ruckleigh School, 63

Saddlers Arms, **14**, 21, 27
St Alphege Church, 41-2, **43-4**, 45,
    52, 67, 85, 86, 87, 99, 106, 108,
    109
St Alphege Church Choir, **45**, 96
St Alphege Fair, 5, 14-5, 94

St Alphege Rectories I-III, 46, 83-4, 91, **101**
St Alphege School, 53
St Augustine's Church, **46**, 47, **48**
St Augustine's School, 57, 59
St Bernard's Grange, 86
St Bernard's Road, **11**
St Catherine's Church, 44
St Francis' Church, 45
St Helen's Church, 46
St James' Church, Shirley, 42-3, 67
St James' Church, Bentley Heath, 44
St Martin's School, 64
St Mary's Church, Hobs Moat, 45-6
St Michael's Church, 46
St Ninian's Church, 49
Sandal's Bridge, **1**, 31
Sanger's Circus, 95
Saracen's Head, 32
Sawmills, 27
Saxtree, Harriet, 19, 23
Saxtree, William, 19
School Lane, 55, 89, **90**
Second World War, 70, 78, 79, 91, 108, 113-21
Seven Star Inn, 104
Sewerage, 67
Sharmans Cross School, 59
Shelly Farm, 13, 122
Shenstone, William, 55
Shipley, Edwin, 51
Shirley, 2, 16, 32, 40
Shopping, 16-25
Short, John, 65
Short, John Holbeche, 44
Sibree, John, 48
Silhill Hall, 9, 75, 81, **82**
Silhill House, **19**, 24, 34
Smith, E. Orford, 66, 67
Smith, Harry Charles, 69
Solihull Board of Guardians, 66, 79
Solihull Brickworks, **27**
Solihull Charity Estate, 52-3, 65
Solihull Clinic, 80
Solihull Constituency, 70
Solihull Council House, Homer Road, 71, 122
Solihull Council House, Poplar Road, 49, 69, 70, 71, 113-4
Solihull County Borough, 71, 122
Solihull & District Synagogue, 51
Solihull Gas Company, 19, 73-4
Solihull Gas Works, 33, 73-4, 114, 118
Solihull Guild of Amateur Bellringers, 87, 96
Solihull Hospital, 79, 117
Solihull Library, 86, 97, 110

Solihull Lodge, 16
Solihull Metropolitan Borough, 72, 122
Solihull Motors, 120
Solihull Municipal Borough, 24, 70-1, 122
Solihull Parkway Hospital, 80
Solihull Races, 104
Solihull Railway Station, 34, 73
Solihull Rural District Council, 40, **66**, 67-8
Solihull Rural Sanitary Authority, 66-7, 73, 74
Solihull School, 52-5
Solihull Society of Arts, 30, 99
Solihull Talking Newspaper, 86
Solihull Union Workhouse, 66, 67, 77, 79, 117
Solihull Urban District Council, 24, 68-70, 71, 113, 115, 122
Solihull Vestry, 65, 67
Solihull Workhouse, 66
Southend, 63, 83
Spelman, Caroline, 73
Square, 106
Station Road, 24, 107
Stewart, Mrs., 19
Stratford Canal, 1
Streetsbrook Road, **2**, 51, 67, 69, 75, 107
Swinburne, Joseph, 109
Symes, Francis, 10

Tainters Green, 25, 89
Tanhouse Farm, 10
Tanworth-in-Arden, 67, 68
Tanyard Cottages, 26
Taylor, Hugh, 104
Thompson, Francis, 67
Totehill, 118
Touchwood, 25, 71, 122
Touchwood Hall, 86-7, 95
Touchwood Hall Close, 86
Townsend, Roy, 113-4
Townshend, Miss, 112
Trades, medieval, 25
Tree School, 63-4
Trinder, Edwin, 79, 108
Trinder, Hugh, 108
Tucker, Christine, 64
Tudor Grange, 91, 117
Tudor Grange Grammar School, 61
Tudor Grange Park, 122
Turchil, 3
Turnpike roads, 31-2

Ulleries Road, 4, 121
Ulverlei, 2, 3, 4, 41, 109

Ulverley Green Road, 4
Union Road, 48, 66, 67, 79

Van Wart, Irving, 6, 15, 61, 63, 83, 86, 95
Victoria: Coronation, 106; Diamond Jubilee, 102, **106**, 107; Golden Jubilee, 107
Village Farm, 13
Vivacious, HMS, 115-6

Walker, Eric, 105
Walker, M., 119
War Memorial, 113
Waring: family, 53, 82; John, 47
Warner: family, 9; Mrs., **8**, **9**
Warwick & Birmingham Canal, 32-3
Warwick County Council, 59, 67, 68, 79
Warwick Road, **1**, **3**, 19, 21, **22**, 23, 25, **26**, 27, **31**, **39**, 49, 51, 66, 68, 74, 75, 79, 86, **88-9**, **92**, 104
Warwick Road Turnpike Trust, 32
Wassell, Richard, 99
Water pump, **72**, 73
Welch, Jesse, 76
Weston, Joseph, 86
Whar Hall Farm, **9**, **10**, 13, 112
White: Neville, 55; William, 110
White Cat Café, 19
White Swan, 32, 34
Whitefields Road, 110
Whitehouse, St John, 76, 78, **106**, 112
Whittington, Joseph, 23
Whittington's grocer's shop, **22**, 23
Widney Manor, 34, 76
Widney Manor Road, 9, 68, 80, 82, 83
Widney Road, 44
Wigley, Caroline Meysey, 16, 84-5
Wigley, family, 7
Wilcox, Doris, 78-9
William I, 3
Williams, 'Cabbie', 38
Wilsdon, Amy, 28; James, 27-8; Leslie, 28-9; Walter, 28-9, 110
Wilsdon & Co Ltd., 28-9, **40**
Wilson, George, 66, 67
Wilson, William 'Gumley', 84-5, 104
Winfield's chemist's shop, 79, 114
Wise, Jacob, 46
Witley Farm, **7**, 9, **10**, **12**, 82
Woods, Courtenay, 96
Wormald, C.O.R., 44, 85, 102, 110
Wormell, C.O.R., 85